African
Safari

Fodor's Travel Publications
New York Toronto London Sydney Auckland

Fodor's African Safari

Editors: Melissa Klurman, Chris Swiac

Writers: David Bristow, Julian Harrison
Editorial Contributors: Carissa Bluestone, Jennifer Paull
Design: Guido Caroti
Cover Photo: Joseph Van Os/The Image Bank/Getty Images

Copyright
Copyright © 2004 by Fodors LLC

Fodor's is a registered trademark of Random House, Inc.

First Edition

ISBN 1–4000–1234–1

ISSN 1541–2865

Important Tip
All details in this book are based on information supplied to us at press time. Changes occur all the time in the travel world, and Fodor's cannot accept responsibility for facts that become outdated or for inadvertent errors or omissions. So **always confirm information when it matters.**

Special Sales
This book is available for special discounts for bulk purchases for sales promotions or premiums. Special editions, including personalized covers, excerpts of existing books, and corporate imprints, can be created in large quantities for special needs. For more information, write to Special Markets/Premium Sales, 1745 Broadway, MD 6-2, New York, NY 10019 or e-mail specialmarkets@randomhouse.com.

PRINTED IN THE UNITED STATES OF AMERICA

10 9 8 7 6 5 4 3 2

Contents

ABOUT THE WRITERS

DAVID BRISTOW is editor of *Getaway*, Africa's leading travel and ecotourism magazine. He has written more than a dozen books about hiking, mountaineering, and the natural history of Southern Africa as well as a number of travel guides. With *Time* magazine photographer Peter Magubane, Bristow co-produced the book *Soweto: Portrait of a City*. His photographs have illustrated several of his books, and he regularly contributes both photographs and stories to international travel and natural-history magazines. Bristow has degrees in journalism and environmental science; he lives in Cape Town with his wife and three children.

JULIAN HARRISON, born and raised in South Africa, started his career in tourism with the South African Tourism Board, accompanying foreign journalists and television crews covering conservation-related issues in wildlife areas. In the United States he has guest lectured at the Smithsonian Institution and George Washington University, among other venues; been a founding member of the United Nations Environment Program's Initiative on Sustainable Tourism Development; and served on the environmental committee of the American Society of Travel Agents and on the North American Advisory Board for South African Tourism. Now the president of Philadelphia-based Premier Tours, he was named to *Condé Nast Traveler* magazine's list of the top 100 travel agents in the United States in 2001, 2002, and 2003.

A Walk on the Wild Side

At the mention of the word *safari,* most people conjure up visions of wildlife: lions roaring in the gathering dusk, antelope bounding across the savanna, a leopard silhouetted by the setting sun. The images never fail to fascinate and draw us in, and having experienced them, you become a changed person. Africa is not a Disney-choreographed show; this wilderness is a real one. In the African bush, wild animals and pre-industrial people live side by side with nature as they have for thousands of years. A safari, or journey, through this terrain reveals the very beginnings of humankind on this planet, the raw paradise where mankind first walked on the earth, living among and pitting his wits against the most savage of beasts. The look, the feel, even the smell of the African bush seep into your soul, and long after you've left, you find yourself missing the landscape with an almost physical yearning.

If I know a song of Africa, of the giraffe, and the African new moon lying on her back, of the ploughs in the fields, and the sweaty faces of the coffee-pickers, does Africa know a song of me?

– Isak Dinesen, *Out of Africa*

INTO AFRICA

The first safaris were taken by Arab and Persian traders across the African continent in the 13th century. Needing a common language to facilitate commerce with local tribes, the traders developed Swahili, an amalgam of African Bantu and Arabic; they used the word *safari* to describe their travels. Nineteenth-century Europeans, exploring and colonizing virtually the whole of sub-Saharan Africa, carving it up in what has come to be referred to as the "scramble for Africa," went off on safari—although their purpose was not trade but the adventure of shooting trophies in the bush so that they could hang the heads on their walls.

Nowadays, the romance of these safaris lingers. And although the word is often used to describe just about any adventure vacation, from a trip to an amusement park to a whale-watching cruise in the Antarctic, a true safari is in Africa, in the bush, with big game all around and without guns. Because Africa is so diverse and so very large—approximately 2½ times the size of the United States—good planning is essential. Still, the challenge is not insurmountable. Once you find out how easy it is to insert yourself into a safari scenario, you may be amazed that you didn't do it sooner. This book is full of pointers; here are a few to get you started.

Embarking

▶ Find someone you trust to help plan your trip. Within the safari business are some of Africa's best-trained professionals, including guides who have the equivalent of a college degree in bush craft—or a lifetime's experience.

▶ Get a little help from your friends. Word-of-mouth advice is the best kind. If you know people who have had a terrific safari, find out what they loved and what to avoid; get their tips on what to pack and what to leave behind; and find out the highlights of their trip.

▶ Try not to pack too much into your itinerary. The African bush moves to a slow drumbeat; don't try to impose a hectic schedule on your time there if you want to experience the hypnotic essence. Game viewing is seldom predictable, and the interactions between animals and their environments are extremely com-

SAFARI SPEAK

The following words and terms are used throughout the book.

- ☐ **ablution blocks:** public bathrooms

- ☐ **banda:** bungalow or hut

- ☐ **Big Five:** buffalo, elephant, leopard, lion, and rhinoceros, collectively

- ☐ **boma:** a fenced-in or roofed eating area

- ☐ **bush:** word for African safari areas; *see* bushveld

- ☐ **bushveld:** general safari area in South Africa, usually with scattered shrubs and trees and lots of game; also referred to as the *bush* or the *veld*

- ☐ **camp:** used interchangeably with *lodge*

- ☐ **campground:** a place used for camping that encompasses several campsites and often includes some shared facilities

- ☐ **campsite:** may or may not be part of a campground

- ☐ **concession:** game-area lease that is granted to a safari company and gives it exclusive access to the land

- ☐ **game guide:** often used interchangeably with *ranger;* usually male

- ☐ **hides:** small, partially camouflaged shelters from which to view game

- ☐ **kraal:** traditional home in Southern Africa

- ☐ **lodge:** accommodation in rustic-yet-stylish tents, rondavels, or lavish suites; prices at lodges include all meals and game-viewing

- **mobile or overland safari:** usually a self-sufficient camping affair set up at a different location (at public or private campgrounds) each night
- **mokoro:** dugout canoe; pluralized as *mekoro*
- **photographic safari:** a game-viewing excursion
- **ranger:** safari guide with vast experience with and knowledge of the bush and the animals that inhabit it; often used interchangeably with *game guide*
- **rest camp:** camp in a national park
- **rondavel:** a traditional thatch-roof hut
- **self-drive safari:** budget-safari option during which you drive, and guide, yourself in a rented vehicle
- **tracker:** works in conjunction with a ranger (mostly in South Africa), spotting animals from a special seat on the front of the four-wheel-drive game-viewing vehicle
- **veld:** a grassland; *see* bushveld
- **vlei:** wetland or marsh

plex. To get even the smallest insight into an area, you have to take the time to observe it. Animals and birds come and go, using almost imperceptible cues for their entrances and their exits. Bottom line: Two nights in one place should be your minimum. Three nights in each of two or more places, depending on how much time you have, is better still.

▶ Choose the right destination. For a first safari, you may want to visit Kruger National Park in South Africa or Serengeti National Park in Tanzania. Regardless of the crowds at these popular destinations, it's here that you're most likely to see the Big Five— lion, leopard, elephant, buffalo, and rhinoceros. On a second or third trip, you may want to take in Namibia, Zambia, or another area that gives you a greater sense of wilderness. Not much can beat the thrill of seeing your first elephant or lion up close in the wild, but once you've been on several safaris, you may want to start focusing on the many other wonders of the African bush—most notably, the birds, the insects, and the plants.

▶ Work with your guides and rangers. The more time you spend with them, the more detailed the information you receive from them will be. Guides and rangers are also more communicative if you show them you already know a little about the area and animal behavior. Although there are no bad questions, rangers may assume that you're less than interested if you repeatedly ask uninformed questions—whether giraffes hunt in packs (an impossibility given that giraffes are herbivores), for example. Insightful questions, such as "Why do giraffes chew bones if they're herbivores?" may inspire your guide to open up and share his knowledge. (Giraffes chew bones for the calcium.)

In choosing to take a safari, you're about to embark on one of the biggest travel adventures of your life. You'll invest time, money, and effort to make sure it goes just right. Planning well is the best way to ensure that you return with memories to last a lifetime—or at least until your next safari. By following the advice in these pages, you'll know that you've taken care of the details. Then you can relax, enjoy, and let the African bush take care of the rest.

– THE EDITORS

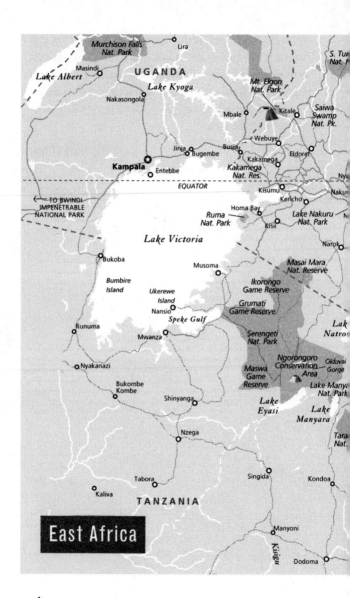

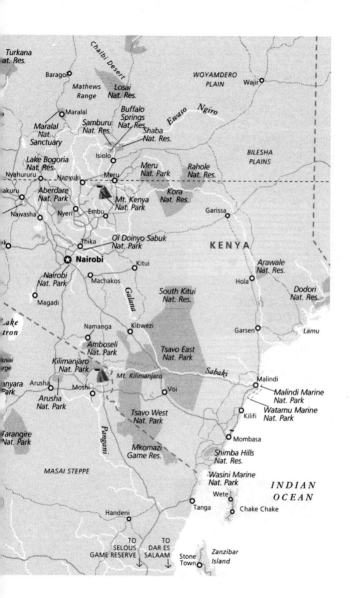

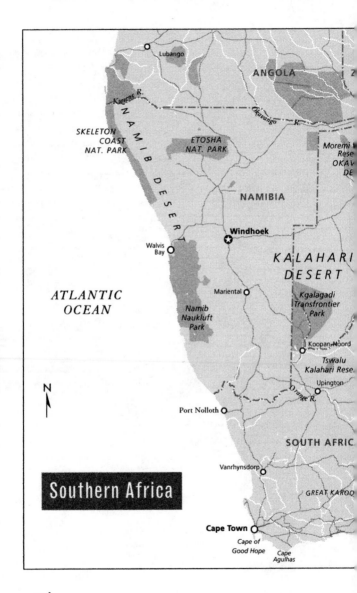

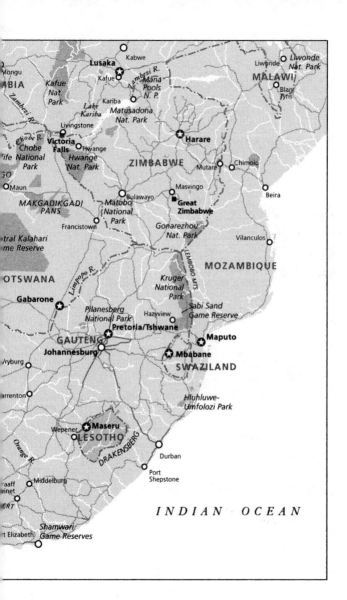

1

Getting Started

It's never too soon to start planning your safari. Africa is both complex and diverse, so you need to consider a multitude of factors when planning your trip: geography, animal migrations, weather, visa requirements, inoculations, and the political stability and general safety of the country (or countries) you want to visit. In addition you must consider your budget, schedule, fitness level, and comfort requirements. Most people start planning a safari six to nine months in advance, which allows time to set a spending limit, choose an itinerary, and organize travel documents.

You can wait and plan the trip over a few weeks, but doing so greatly increases your chances of being closed out of the places you really want to see. Indeed, planning your trip 12 months in advance isn't unreasonable, especially if you want to travel during peak season—November through February in South Africa, July through September or October elsewhere—and have your heart set on a particular lodge.

Start planning for your safari the way you would any trip. Read travel books about the areas that most interest you. Rent wildlife documentaries to get a feel for the places you want to visit. Talk to people who have been on a similar trip or visit an online chat room to contact people who have gone on safari. Get inspired.

DOING YOUR HOMEWORK

Deciding which places to see and choosing the safari operator in whose hands you'll place your trip are the most important things you need to do. Each country, each wildlife area, even each game guide is different in countenance and personality, and part of the joy of a safari is discovering this uniqueness. Your research will help you choose the safari experience that's right for you as well as add depth to your safari experience.

Did you know that elephants communicate via ultrasound, even when separated by several miles of dense bush? Or that giraffes don't make any sound at all (at least not one that's been recorded)? If you saw a scorpion, would you know that one with small pincers and a thick tail is dangerous and that one with large pincers and a thin tail isn't?

You can learn a lot from specialized field guides, which have in-depth coverage about topics from flora and fauna to animal behavior and game tracking, and a good guidebook gives you basic history and geography. It would take a lifetime to learn firsthand about everything that lives and flourishes in the bush, though, so having a professional guide or tracker with you on safari is invaluable. Many guides (nearly all of whom are men) were born in these areas and have completed intensive studies in animal behavior and environmental sciences. You'll give your guide a better idea of your interests if you study beforehand and can show him that you've learned something in advance; he in turn will be able to tailor the information he gives you to better suit your needs. If you don't prepare in advance, your guide may assume your interest is superficial and hold back on the level of description he goes into.

Travel Agents & Safari Operators

There's no substitute for a knowledgeable tour operator or travel agent who specializes in Africa. These specialists look out for your best interests and are aware of trends and developments. A good tour operator or travel agent is indispensable as backup in the rare instance when something goes wrong.

The age of Internet bookings is upon us, with real-time inventories and Web sites where you can find bargain packages, book a specific airplane seat, even pick

SAFARI PLANNING TIMELINE

Six Months to One Year Ahead

- ☐ Begin to daydream about your safari.
- ☐ Research destinations and options and make a list of the sights you want to see.
- ☐ Start a safari file to keep track of relevant information.
- ☐ Set a budget.
- ☐ Consult guidebooks and narrow your choices.
- ☐ Search the Internet. Post questions on bulletin boards.
- ☐ Contact a travel agent to start firming up details.
- ☐ Choose your destination and make your reservations.
- ☐ Buy travel insurance.

Three to Six Months Ahead

- ☐ Find out which travel documents you need.
- ☐ Apply for a passport, or renew yours if it's due to expire within six months of travel time.
- ☐ Confirm whether your destination requires visas and certified health documents.
- ☐ Arrange vaccinations or medical clearances.
- ☐ Research malaria precautions.
- ☐ Book excursions, tours, and side trips.

One to Three Months Ahead

- ☐ Create a packing checklist.
- ☐ Fill prescriptions for anti-malarial and regular medications. Buy mosquito repellent.

- [ ] Shop for safari clothing and equipment.
- [ ] Arrange a kennel for pets and a house sitter.

One Month Ahead

- [ ] Get copies of any prescriptions and ensure you have enough of any needed medicine to last you a few days longer than your trip.
- [ ] Confirm international flights directly and lodging reservations and transfers with your travel agent.
- [ ] Buy additional guidebooks and light reading.

Three Weeks Ahead

- [ ] Using your packing list, start buying items you don't have. Update the list as you go.
- [ ] Take care of any clothes that need mending or other items that require attention.

Two Weeks Ahead

- [ ] Purchase traveler's checks and some local currency. Collect small denominations of U.S. currency ($1 and $5) for tips.
- [ ] Get ready to pack; remember bag size and weight restrictions.

One Week Ahead

- [ ] Suspend newspaper and mail delivery.
- [ ] List contact numbers and other details for your house sitter.
- [ ] Check anti-malarial prescriptions to see whether you need to start taking medication now.
- [ ] Dry-clean and wash clothes.

- ☐ Arrange transportation to the airport.
- ☐ Make two copies of your passport's data page. Leave one copy, and a copy of your itinerary, with someone at home; pack the other separately from your passport.

A Few Days Ahead

- ☐ Take pets to the kennel.
- ☐ Pack.
- ☐ Reconfirm flights.
- ☐ Buy snacks and gum for the plane.

One Day Ahead

- ☐ Enable your e-mail "out of office" message.
- ☐ Check destination weather reports.
- ☐ Make a last check of your house and go through your travel checklist one final time.

the bed you want in a particular lodge. Some people love to bargain hunt, find the best deal, haggle, make mistakes along the way, and learn from them, but it's important to remember that a bargain price may get you a bargain experience.

Although the Internet is useful for booking in Europe and other destinations with a sophisticated travel infrastructure in place, it's not an efficient option for Africa, where logistical nightmares are usually the norm in trying to piece together an itinerary. You may manage to successfully put together a trip on your own, but you'll be just that—on your own—once in your safari destination. Faced with a challenge such as a canceled flight, or something more drastic—like the floods that swept through South Africa's Sabi Sand region a few years ago—you won't have anyone back home to help you with new arrangements. Well-established and -connected safari specialists (a general term for a safari outfitter or African-tour operator) can take advantage of long-standing business relationships to secure the assistance their clients need, whether it be last-minute transportation or lodging or a way to communicate with family back home. Furthermore, many safari lodges, such as those run by Wilderness Safaris, require individuals to reserve through an African-tour operator or a travel agent.

Before you entrust your trip to an agent, however, you want to determine the extent of his or her knowledge as well as the level of enthusiasm he or she has for the destination. There are as many travel companies claiming to specialize in Africa as there are hippos in the Zambezi, so it's especially important to determine which operators and agents are up to the challenge.

After choosing a tour operator or travel agent, it's a good idea to discuss with him or her the logistics and details of the itinerary so you know what to expect each day.

Ask questions about lodging, even if you're traveling on a group tour. A lodge that is completely open to the elements, providing an exquisite view of Mt. Kilimanjaro from your bed, may be a highlight for some travelers and terrifying for others, particularly at night when a lion roars nearby.

A number of professionals in the African travel industry provide specialized services.

▶ **African safari outfitter.** Also referred to as a ground operator, this type of outfitter is a company in Africa that provides logistical support to a U.S.–based tour operator by seeing to the details of your safari. An outfitter might charter flights, pick you up at the airport, and take you on game-viewing trips, for example. Some outfitters own or manage safari lodges. In addition, an outfitter communicates changing trends and developments in the region to tour operators and serves as your on-site contact in cases of illness, injury, and other unexpected situations.

▶ **African-tour operator.** Based in the United States, this type of company specializes in tours and safaris to Africa and works with a safari outfitter that provides support on the ground. Start dates and itineraries are set for some trips offered by the operator, but customized vacations can be arranged. Travelers usually find out about these trips through retail travel agents.

▶ **Air consolidator.** A consolidator promotes and sells plane tickets to Africa, usually concentrating on one or a few airlines to ensure a large volume of sales with those particular carriers. The airlines provide greatly reduced airfares to the consolidator, who in turn adds a markup and resells them directly to you.

> **Retail travel agent.** In general, a travel agent sells trip packages directly to consumers. In most cases an agent doesn't have a geographical specialty. When called on to arrange a trip to Africa, the travel agent turns to an African-tour operator for details.

In addition, inquire about the amount of time you'll spend with other travelers. If you're planning a safari honeymoon, find out how many meals will be communal and ask about honeymoon packages.

WHAT'S YOUR BUDGET?

There's no simple answer to the question of how much money to spend on a safari. It's like the old riddle "How long is a piece of string?" (The answer: Any length, depending on the piece of string in question.) When setting a safari budget, you must consider how much you want to spend or how much you can afford.

You can have a low-budget trip in Zimbabwe, where the U.S. dollar is very strong, or spend a great deal of money in one of the small, exclusive camps in Botswana. Almost every market has high-priced options as well as some very economical ones. When planning your safari budget, keep in mind three main factors: airfare, the actual safari costs, and extras.

Across the Wide Ocean

Africa is a long way from the United States, and airfares can be steep. Airline consolidators that specialize in airfares to Africa, however, are often in a position to offer extremely competitive fares, at times even less than US$1,000 round-trip. Given the distance between the two continents and the resulting flying time, the fares regularly represent the best value-for-money airfares compared with any other route in the world.

Ideally, a round-trip economy fare from the East Coast of the United States to South Africa is approximately US$1,100 in low season and about US$1,500 in high season, excluding tax. The cost varies from airline to airline, with dramatic differences in business-class airfares. American Express offers its platinum-card holders a two-for-one deal in business class on certain airlines. If booking your flight yourself, shop around and call consolidators before settling on a price.

Before and after your safari, you'll have to spend at least one night in either Johannesburg or Nairobi, depending on your safari destination. The only direct flights offered at this writing from the United States to Africa are with South African Airways, which flies from New York or Atlanta to Johannesburg and Cape Town in South Africa, with connecting feeder flights that head as far north as Entebbe in Uganda and Nairobi in Kenya.

Direct flights from New York and Atlanta take approximately 15 hours. Some flights out of New York

Don't forward a deposit to a safari specialist until you have considered his or her answers to these questions. (Where applicable, preferred answers follow in parentheses.)

☐ Do you handle Africa exclusively? (Yes.)

☐ How many years have you been selling tours in Africa? (At least three.)

☐ Are you or any of the staff native to the continent? (Someone should be.)

☐ To which professional organizations do you belong? For example, the American Society of Travel Agents (ASTA) or the United States Tour Operators Association (USTOA)? (Specialist should belong to one or more.)

☐ Can you provide a reference list of past clients? (If not, go elsewhere.)

☐ How often do you and your staff visit Africa? (At least annually.)

☐ What sort of support (business relationships) do you have in Africa?

☐ Do you charge a fee? (Most agents and operators make their money through such fees, usually $150–$600 per booking.)

☐ What is your cancellation policy?

☐ Can you handle arrangements from start to finish, including flights? (Yes.)

stop en route in Ilha Do Sol, in the Cape Verde Islands, or Dakar, in Senegal. Flights within the United States to the gateways of New York and Atlanta are plentiful as a result of the code-share agreement between South African Airways and Delta Airlines. South African Airways is recommended, particularly for travel to safaris in the Southern Africa region, because it's the most modern and wide-reaching airline operating in Southern and East Africa and because its standards equal those of the top international carriers. Within East and Southern Africa, the next-best alternatives are Comair, operated by British Airways, and Nationwide Airlines. Nationwide is affiliated with Virgin Airlines and has new, modern planes and efficient service.

Virgin Atlantic, British Airways, Lufthansa, and KLM, among others, offer regularly scheduled service to Africa from most major cities in the United States via corresponding cities in Europe. Traveling this way often results in two overnight flights with lengthy layovers in Europe. However, this routing does offer the opportunity to break up a trip with a stopover in any one of a number of European countries. Because there are no direct flights from the United States to East and Central Africa, travel via Europe is generally recommended for safaris in these destinations and usually gives you more flight options.

Luxury Safaris
The most popular safari-planning option is to book with a tour operator and stay in private lodges, which are owned and run by an individual or company

rather than a government or country. These lodges, at times referred to as camps and often luxurious, offer accommodation in stylishly rustic tents; thatched huts called rondavels; or, sometimes, as in South Africa, lavish suites with everything from air-conditioning to plunge pools. Prices at these lodges include all meals and, in many cases, most or all alcoholic beverages, as well as two three- to five-hour-long game-viewing expeditions a day. Occasionally high-end lodges offer extra services such as spa treatments, boat trips, or special-occasion meals served alfresco somewhere in the bush. Prices range from US$350 to US$1,200 per person a night sharing a double room; if you travel alone, you have to pay a single supplement because all safari-lodge rooms are doubles. Safari lodges with unique or especially extravagant facilities or options charge accordingly—up to US$1,500 per person per night. Those who can afford private lodges say they're worth every cent for the spectacular game viewing, the knowledgeable guides, the well-prepared food, and the attention to detail.

Safaris on a Shoestring

Don't let a tight budget deter you from a safari adventure. There are many opportunities for big-game experiences outside the luxury lodges. Your least expensive option is to choose one of the public game parks in Southern Africa—Kruger National Park in South Africa, for example, or Etosha National Park in Namibia—where you drive yourself and self-cater (shop for and prepare all meals yourself). The price of this type of trip is approximately one-tenth of that for private, fully inclusive lodges.

Mobile safaris are another option. On this type of trip, travel is by four-wheel-drive vehicle (often something that looks like a bus), and you sleep in tents at public or private campsites. Botswana is one inexpensive mobile-safari destination. Self-drive safaris are popular with locals, but you need to be self-sufficient and bush-savvy to travel this way.

A rental car costs approximately US$300 a week, without fuel (about 50¢ per gallon) but including insurance. Rates for the camps in national parks, called rest camps, start at about US$40 a day for a two-bed rondavel and go up to US$60 for a four-bed bungalow. Budget about US$5 for breakfast, US$8 for lunch, and US$12 for dinner per person for each day on the trip. You also need to figure in entrance charges to the parks (starting at US$5 a person per day).

Alternatively, several safari operators offer three- to five-day safari packages that start and end in major cities such as Johannesburg and Windhoek. Drifters, an African-tour operator, has a five-day safari to Kruger National Park priced at US$570 per person. Drifters also offers fly-in safaris through Zambia, Zimbabwe, and Botswana. Prices range from US$1,375 for 8 days to US$1,950 for 13 days. These are incredible values, but there are a few caveats: you have to be between the ages of 18 and 55, and accommodation is often in small tents you pitch yourself.

Other, slightly higher priced options include private lodges that may lack pools or some other upscale amenities found at luxury camps but that are in wonderful locations and have knowledgeable and helpful staff. These lodges include Drifters Game Lodge in the Balulue Nature Reserve and Akeru Camp in the Timbavati Game Reserve—both near Kruger National Park—and Mashatu Game Reserve in the Tuli Block of Botswana; they cost US$140 to US$220 a night per person and include all meals plus game-viewing activities with an experienced guide.

If you book into a private lodge off-season, you can save a bundle of money. Many lodges in the Sabi Sand area of South Africa, for example, usually cost about US$500 per person a night during the high season but drops to approximately US$300 a night during the slower months of July and August.

The Extras

You'll have other expenses besides airfare and safari costs, including tips, medications, and film and other sundries. For ease of travel, and to help you adjust to jet lag, plan to stay at a city hotel on your first and last nights in Africa. Expect to pay from US$75 for basic accommodations to US$250 a night in the most luxurious hotels.

Plan to spend, on average, US$5 to US$15 a day (per traveler) on gratuities. In South Africa, tips are on the higher end of this range and usually are paid in rand (the local currency); you may also use U.S. dollars for tips, however. Elsewhere in Southern Africa, U.S. currency is preferable, but tips paid in rand may also be accepted. In East Africa, tips are paid in U.S. dollars or the local currency.

A two-week course of anti-malarial medication costs between US$10 and US$100, depending on your health insurance. Stock up on film before you head out into the bush; a roll of regular print film costs about US$3 to US$4 in South Africa and soars to US$8–US$12 in a safari camp. And don't forget to put money aside for souvenirs; you'll undoubtedly want to take home reminders of your trip.

SPECIAL CONSIDERATIONS

Children on Safari

If your children are 12 or older, a safari as a family will probably be one of the highlights of life together. Being away from computers, televisions, radios, telephones, and video games may take a day or two of adjustment, but discovering a group of frolicking baboons outside the tent door or following a lion as it stalks its prey should quickly liberate your offspring from their usual attachments. Children who love dinosaurs are enthralled when they see a lumbering rhino up close or the reticulated neck of a giraffe, definite remains of those long-ago creatures. And the fascinating details of daily sights in the bush—a dung beetle rolling its heavy load, the resplendent plumage of a lilac-breasted roller, a baby warthog trotting after its long-nosed mother—should give you plenty to talk about for many years to come.

Most safari operators and private game reserves don't accept children under a certain age, usually under 8, but sometimes the age limit is as high as 12. This age limit is largely for safety reasons. Animals often respond, not in a positive manner, to something that is younger, slower, or smaller than they are. And even though you might think your six- or seven-year-old adores all sorts of animals and bugs, you'd be surprised how overwhelmed kids can become, out of the comfort of their home and backyard, by the size and multitude of African insects and wildlife.

Take into account, also, that when you're following a strange schedule and getting in and out of small planes, safari vehicles, boats, and the like with other people whom you probably won't know, there often is no time to deal with recalcitrant children—and fussing will, you can be guaranteed, annoy the other people in your plane or lodge, who have spent a great deal of money for what may be a once-in-a-lifetime safari trip.

One option, if you can afford it, is to book a private safari where no other people are involved and you dictate the schedule. Many private lodges will rent you the entire property for the length of your stay; this is often the only way these camps allow children under age 8 on safari. At the very least, a camp will require that you pay for a private safari vehicle and guide if you have children under 12. Be advised that, even if you're renting the whole camp, babies and toddlers still aren't allowed out on game-viewing trips.

One great family option is to stay with Conservation Corporation Africa (CC Africa), a safari operator with children's programs at several of their upscale camps throughout Southern and East Africa. While you follow your own program, your kids pursue their own wilderness activities; you all meet up later for meals and other activities.

A much cheaper alternative is also one of the most enjoyable for a safari as a family: a self-driving trip where you stay at national parks. No destination is better in this regard than Kruger National Park in South Africa, where there are comfortable accommodations and lots of other families around. You'll be able to set your own schedule, rent a cottage large enough for the entire family, and buy and prepare food you know your children will eat.

It's best not to visit malarial areas with children under age 10. Young kidneys are especially vulnerable to both the effects of malaria and the side effects of malaria prophylactics. You might opt to practice stringent nonchemical preventive measures, but know the risks: malaria's effects on young children are much worse than they are on older people.

Going on safari with babies also isn't recommended. Some lodges, such as those at Mala Mala, provide babysitting service for infants, but babies aren't allowed

SHOULD YOU TAKE THE KIDS?

Consider the following if you're thinking about bringing children to a private safari lodge:

▶ Are they afraid of the dark? A safari camp that runs on generator-powered batteries will have minimal lights at night.

▶ Are they startled easily? Large animals may come quite close to rooms or tents or near safari vehicles.

▶ Are they comfortable with strangers? Most meals at safari lodges are at communal tables, and shared six-seat planes are the basic form of transportation between remote safari camps.

▶ Are they troubled by bugs? The African bush can be filled with moths as big as small birds as well as a host of other flying and crawling insects.

▶ Are they picky eaters? Meals are usually buffet style and food for camps is often ordered at least a month in advance, so your child's favorite food may not be available.

out in safari vehicles. The sound of an infant crying puts most predators on alert—dangerous to other passengers as well as the child. Keep in mind also that the bush is often a hot and dusty place with little in the way of baby-friendly amenities. You'd have to bring all your own supplies, and if something were to go wrong there would be no way to get immediate help until a flight could be arranged.

My children were three, five, and seven years old when I took them to Africa. We chose Kenya because

TRAVEL LOG children of all ages are welcomed at most safari camps

there, and transportation is provided in closed minibuses equipped with a roof viewing hatch. These vehicles, unlike the open ones used in Southern Africa, provided peace of mind because it was far less likely for one of the children to tumble out accidentally while viewing lions or other dangerous animals. We customized our trip in order to have the vehicle to ourselves; my daughter, the youngest, could nap across the back seat during a game drive so we didn't have to return to the lodge. Our itinerary was designed with the children's health in mind; we chose parks at an altitude high enough to greatly reduce—and, in many cases, eliminate completely—the likelihood of contracting malaria or any other diseases. Also, much thought went into planning day-to-day activities, not only to provide diversity but also to avoid driving for long periods. Our activities included going with Samburu tribesmen into the bush to collect wild honey and eat it from the comb; catching and releasing fish among hippos in the river; visiting remote villages where, among other things, the children got to milk goats; and going to the riverbed in the morning to make plaster casts of prints left by animals the previous night. The ultimate highlight was an overnight camping safari with camels.

–Rosemarie H., Philadelphia

People with Disabilities

Having a disability doesn't mean you cannot go on safari. It's important, however, to plan carefully to ensure that your needs can be adequately met. South African lodges, especially the high-end private ones, are the easiest to navigate and have the fewest steps. Keep in mind that all-terrain 4×4 vehicles don't have seat belts, so you need enough muscle control to keep yourself upright while the vehicle bumps along the unpaved roads. Getting in and out of these elevated vehicles can also be challenging. Mala Mala Game Reserve in South Africa is completely accessible and even has specially equipped four-wheel-drive safari vehicles with harness seat belts.

Gay & Lesbian Travelers

Southern and East Africa are largely conservative, and this orientation informs attitudes toward same-sex couples. In South Africa, by far the most tolerant country in the region, homosexuality is legal and the constitution covers gay and lesbian rights. In Cape Town, which has a fairly large gay population, and other parts of the country, the so-called Pink Route highlights gay-friendly and/or gay-owned lodgings. Gay people should be circumspect elsewhere, however; homosexuality is technically illegal in Botswana, Kenya, Malawi, Namibia, Tanzania, Uganda, Zaire, and Zimbabwe.

Health Restrictions

Traveling on safari with an ailment can be recommended only if sufficient precautions have been taken. Before you book your trip, consult your physician and make sure your medical requirements can be accommodated by the lodges you choose. In addition, ask your doctor several weeks before departure to determine if your current medication might react to malaria prophylactics or any other shots you may be considering. Soon after you book your trip, have your travel agent or tour operator inform the various camps where you'll be staying about your specific situation and medications. It goes without saying that comprehensive travel insurance, including health insurance and emergency medical transportation, is a must.

Older Travelers

Safaris everywhere welcome older travelers. However, before you book a safari, find out as many details as possible about how taxing a trip might be both physically and mentally. Consider the types of accommodations (for example, find out whether a lodge is built on an incline or has many stairs, and whether bathrooms have grab bars) as well as how much time will be spent in the elements, such as in the hot sun where it's easy to dehydrate, and whether there are daily activities such as canoeing that are physically challenging. For travelers older than 55, Elderhostel arranges a number of annual educational trips to both East and Southern Africa that consider special needs.

2

Where & When to Go

To put it mildly, Africa is a big place. The second-largest continent after Asia, Africa is made up of 45 countries, and nearly 1,000 languages are spoken within its borders. The continent has five geographic areas. Northern Africa is bordered by the intensely blue Mediterranean Sea but is largely dry and barren, covered mostly by the Sahara. West Africa is part Sahel—the semi-arid area of the Sahara that gives way first to savanna, or subtropical grasslands, and then to jungle somewhere in northern Congo. Central Africa is an enigmatic jungle land. Southern and East Africa are fairly similar to each other, covered by savanna and by the archetypal endless African plains.

African Safari focuses on the savanna region in Southern and East Africa, the land of wide plains and big game. Botswana, Malawi, Namibia, South Africa, Zambia, and Zimbabwe are in Southern Africa; Kenya, Tanzania, and Uganda are in East Africa. All are known for their unique game-viewing opportunities and beautiful landscapes.

The areas covered in this book are in the Southern Hemisphere, and their seasons are opposite to those in the Northern Hemisphere. Winter runs from about June through September, spring from October through November, summer from December through March, and fall from April through May.

SOUTHERN AFRICA

The region known as Southern Africa encompasses the bottom tip of the African continent. Moving from the southernmost part clockwise, the area includes South Africa, Namibia, Botswana, Zambia, Malawi, and Zimbabwe. Although each country is distinct, these neighboring states share a similar culture as well as close economic and social ties. Natural habitats, on the other hand, are diverse, ranging from harsh desert to montane (the green lower areas of mountains),

CONCESSIONS

In Southern and East Africa, game areas bordering national parks and other tracts of wilderness have been sectioned into private areas and leased to safari companies who then have the exclusive right to build game lodges and traverse the area for game drives or other activities. This concession system is now being extended into the national parks themselves, as government conservation authorities let private operators handle the tourism side of the business.

bushveld (areas of dense scrub brush that make up most safari areas; also referred to as the bush or veld) to subtropical forest. Modern cities, European-style vineyards, and vast tracts of wilderness sit comfortably side by side. The formation of transfrontier or "peace parks"—brave new worlds of conservation—is creating huge game corridors along natural lines that most often form national borders. Kgalagadi Transfrontier Park, which straddles South Africa and Botswana, and the much larger Limpopo Transfrontier Park, which links game-rich areas in South Africa, Zimbabwe, and Mozambique, are the two most important parks. The rule of thumb in Southern Africa is that winter is best for seeing game, but the season is also dry and dusty; summers are best for birds and to see the grasslands and woodlands at their green best.

Botswana

In the 1970s Botswana was one of the premier hunting destinations in Africa, and photographic safaris, as purely game-viewing excursions are now called, were virtually unheard of. Since the 1970s, however, attitudes toward hunting and conservation have changed, and today photographic safaris are the norm. Along with this change in sentiment came a shift in the government's tourism policies that has encouraged low-volume, high-end tourism. This approach allows game land to continue to pay for itself but not at the expense of the native wildlife. As a result, Botswana is the most expensive safari destination in Southern Africa, but one that's idyllically uncrowded.

Although Botswana for the most part often looks dusty and hard-bitten, it's an economic anomaly because in per-capita terms it's one of the world's wealthiest nations, with among the biggest foreign-currency reserves. The money comes mainly from two huge diamond mines and, to a lesser extent, from cattle ranching and tourism. Africa's "quiet democracy," Botswana has had no debilitating political turmoil in its modern history. In fact the U.S. State Department calls it "a model for stability in Africa."

A vast geological depression known as the Kalahari Basin cuts across Botswana, which is landlocked. Often referred to as a desert, the Kalahari Basin is actually arid savanna with one great miracle: a river that, instead of searching for the sea, ends in a basin, creating a wonderland of inland waterways called the Okavango

Delta. Northeast of the delta are Savuti and Chobe, seasonal flood-and-famine areas. Chobe is known for its enormous but controversial elephant herds—modern conservation has allowed the populations to grow to be larger than the land can support, thereby reducing the rain forest along the Chobe River to scrub since the 1980s and '90s.

About 90% of Botswana's population lives in a few large towns along the southeastern border, foremost the capital, Gaborone, and then Francistown. The safari area is largely in the far north, which is sparsely populated and served by the frontier town of Maun.

Because the delta has nothing more than rudimentary dirt roads, six-seat Cessna Stationair planes, measuring 28 feet from tip to tail, usually transport you from lodge to lodge. You can travel between some lodges by boat, and, in a few cases, by *mokoro,* or dugout canoe, pluralized as *mekoro. Mekoro* trips are available at about half the lodges; these lodges have shallow channels that allow passage between the large lagoons.

You can visit Botswana more cheaply on a mobile safari, during which you travel by modified bus or safari truck and stay in a self-pitch tent, but you won't be able to enter the private reserves, where the game is densest. Although self-drive camping safaris are popular with locals, you need to be fully self-sufficient and bush-wise to travel this way.

WHEN TO GO Winter, roughly July through October, is the dry season, when grass and bush cover are minimal; animals are easiest to spot during this high-season period. Although winter days are warm—70°F to 85°F—nights can be cold, down around 35°F.

Summer starts in December and runs through March. The days are hot—85°F to 100°F—but night temperatures sometimes cool slightly. The rains fall from late November through February, generally in the form of afternoon thundershowers. When these showers turn into electrical storms, the weather show can rival the most elaborate fireworks display. The threat of malaria is highest during the wet months, when mosquitoes breed. (Some 95% of malaria cases in Botswana occur December through May.) Although summer is considered off-season, the vegetation is green and lush at this time, and the decrease in visitors means you generally have the place to yourself.

The shoulder months of June and November are considered mostly low-season and are great times to view game at much-reduced costs.

Chobe National Park

The cornerstone of Botswana's game reserves is the extensive Chobe National Park, which includes the Chobe River area, the wide-open plains of Savuti, and the riverine woodlands and waterways of Linyanti and Selinda reserves. Whereas the Chobe River has the greatest concentrations of elephants in Africa, Savuti to the south—between Chobe and Moremi—is famous for its lions and hyenas. In August through

October, when water is scarce and animals need to come to the river to drink, elephant populations reach enormous proportions, and you can see anywhere from 400 to 800 elephants in a day. Unfortunately, the land can't always sustain these huge herds; in some places, decades of elephant protection have led to the almost total destruction of the area's once-extensive riverine forests.

Game spotting in Chobe is done mainly on organized drives, with fewer walking options than in other Botswana parks. However, private safari operators with the appropriate licenses can take you walking in the bush. Also here are several game-viewing hides (small, semi-camouflaged shelters), where you can disembark from your vehicle and sit to wait for and watch what comes to drink from the water holes and rivers. Activities in the Chobe fringe, where almost all of the lodges are located, include game drives in open vehicles during both the day and evening and river cruises to view wildlife at the water's edge; the sunset cruises are simply magical. Game drives aren't permitted after dark, a factor to consider when you're deciding where to stay.

ACCOMMODATION IN CHOBE Within the park perimeters are three camping sites (Nogatsaa, Tjinga, and Savuti); Mababe Game Scout Camp; private Natural Habitat campsites, which are used by mobile safaris; and three private lodges, (CC Africa's Savute Elephant Camp and Desert & Delta's Savute Safari

SAFARI HIGH & LOW SEASONS

	SUMMER				AUTUMN
	Dec.	Jan.	Feb.	Mar.	Apr.
Southern Africa					
Botswana	Lo/LR	Lo/LR	Lo/LR	Lo/LR	Lo/LR
Malawi	Lo/LR	Lo/LR	Lo/LR	Lo/LR	Sh
Namibia	Lo/LR	Lo/LR	Lo/LR	Lo/LR	Hi
South Africa	Hi/LR	Hi/LR	Hi/LR	Sh	Sh
Zambia	Sh/LR	Lo/HR	Lo/HR	Lo/HR	Sh/LR
Zimbabwe	Lo/LR	Lo/LR	Lo/LR	Sh	Sh
East Africa					
Kenya	Lo/HR	Hi	Hi	Hi	Lo/HR
Tanzania	Lo/HR	Hi	Hi	Hi	Lo/HR
Uganda	Sh	Sh	Sh	Lo/HR	Lo/HR

KEY
Lo = Low season
Hi = High season
Sh = Shoulder season
LR = Light rain
HR = Heavy rain

Lodge and Chobe Game Lodge, where Richard Burton and Elizabeth Taylor remarried). Most lodges are just outside the park's boundaries; these tend to be upscale and offer evening drives as well as daytime ones.

The Savuti-Linyanti area has mostly Okavango-style tented lodges and camps. Several large hotels, which lack a true game-reserve feel, also serve the Chobe River area. Although these hotels won't put you as

| | WINTER* | | | | | SPRING | |
May	June	July	Aug.	Sept.	Oct.	Nov.
Sh	Sh	Hi	Hi	Hi	Hi	Sh
Hi	Hi	Hi	Hi	Hi	Hi	Sh/LR
Hi	Hi	Hi	Hi	Hi	Hi	Lo/LR
Lo	Lo	Lo	Lo	Sh	Sh	Hi/LR
Sh/LR	Hi	Hi	Hi	Hi	Hi	Sh/LR
Sh	Sh	Hi	Hi	Hi	Hi	Lo/LR
Lo/HR	Lo/HR	Hi	Hi	Hi	Hi	Lo/HR
Lo/HR	Lo/HR	Hi	Hi	Hi	Hi	Lo/HR
Lo/HR	Hi	Hi	Hi	Hi	Lo/HR	Lo/HR

*Winter is usually high season throughout safari areas because it's the driest time of year and game is easiest to spot. The exception is South Africa, where high season is linked with the summer vacation schedules of South Africans.

close to the natural surroundings as smaller lodges or tented camps, their design and decor retain a close association with the bush.

Moremi Safaris & Tours explores the disappearing hunter-gatherer culture of the central Kalahari, linking a stay at Xakanaxa on the edge of the Okavango's permanent waterways with a trip to Deception Valley Lodge deep in the Kalahari, where Bushmen still live and practice their time-old bush craft. You even have the opportunity to go tracking with a Bushman hunting party.

Moremi Wildlife Reserve

Moremi is a seamless extension of the Okavango Delta both as an ecosystem and as a tourist destination. Moremi abuts the Okavango's eastern edge, a 1,100-square-mi triangle extending well into the permanent delta and covering the extraordinary Chief's Island. Although the delta in general is a marvel, Moremi is where all its elements are best concentrated, and it's one of the few safari destinations where you're almost guaranteed to see large numbers of game on almost every outing. Its pristine wilderness of water and land, renowned for its beauty, shelters a profusion of wildlife, including enormous prides of lions and herds of elephants as well as buffalo, leopards, and rarer species such as wild dogs and cheetahs. Rhinoceroses, which no longer exist naturally in Botswana (where their numbers were never great), are being slowly reintroduced and closely monitored as the possible nucleus of a breeding program for the area. Within the park boundaries, at the Mombo or Little Mombo camps, you're limited to morning and late-afternoon game drives, as reserve rules prohibit drives after dark, walking safaris, and boating. If you stay outside the reserve borders, at Xigera Camp or Camp Moremi, your range of available activities expands to include night drives, mokoro and powerboat trips, walking with a guide, and watching game from several hides that have been erected in the area near water holes and rivers;

WHAT ARE THE BIG FIVE?

When the trophy hunters of safari lore went on safari in Africa in the 19th century, the hunt was for heads to hang on their walls. The hunters discovered, in the course of their journeys, that five animals were much more dangerous than others; these animals then became the most desirable trophies. Although the only hunting you'll be doing on safari is for the perfect picture, and another 150 equally interesting species will be all around you, the Big Five will still be referred to throughout your travels in Africa.

☐ **Buffalo.** In a herd, buffalo take flight at the first opportunity. However, lonely old bulls cast out of the herd are dangerous because they're on the defensive. Beware a wounded old bull, for it will hunt you to your death, even if you're not the one who injured it.

☐ **Elephants.** Don't ever be fooled into thinking the largest land animals are slow-witted or slow-footed. An angry elephant is much quicker than either a rhinoceros or a hippopotamus, and if it's cantankerous, as many old bulls are, an elephant can actually track you.

☐ **Leopards.** Although smaller than lions, leopards are far more cunning. A leopard wounded or protecting its young is a wily opponent.

☐ **Lions.** They may seem like the laziest of animals, often sleeping most of the day, but when they move, they can do so with unbelievable speed and power.

☐ **Rhinoceroses.** They are antediluvian, near-sighted, and usually bad tempered. The larger white (square-lipped) species is a grassland grazer and relatively harmless; the black (hook-lipped) rhinoceros, which browses mostly in dense bush, is to be feared and avoided. It will often attack on sight.

fishing is also an option, and some lodges specialize in fly-fishing for tiger fish and pike.

ACCOMMODATION IN MOREMI The permanent safari tents used in the Okavango Delta are also found here. However, when you read "tent," don't for a moment think of scout camp. These tents are room-size structures, usually set on teak decks under shade trees, with proper beds, stylish chairs and tables, clothes closets, and en-suite bathrooms. Sometimes there's an additional shower surrounded by reeds and romantically open to the sky. Mombo and Little Mombo (both Wilderness Safaris properties, as is Xigera), in particular, feel like romantic oases in the middle of the bush. Camp Moremi is a Desert & Delta Safaris property.

The Okavango Delta

The inland delta, completely surrounded by the arid Kalahari savanna, has been called a sea of land and land of water. When inundated, the delta encompasses some 6,000 square mi of waterways, with forest-fringed and palm-filled islands abutting crystal-clear, lily-filled lagoons; it's arguably the greatest natural sanctuary left in Africa today and is home to the greatest number of animal, bird, and plant species in the Southern Hemisphere. The area is accessible only by light aircraft and, in the drier seasons, by some four-wheel-drive vehicles. You can take game drives in open vehicles, walk with local guides on the islands in search of animals, go powerboating in the larger channels, and fish for tiger fish and bream (also known as tilapia). The highlight of any journey to the Okavango is a mokoro trip, where you are poled through reed-lined channels by one of the local Bai-Yei boatmen. The boatmen fill you in on the small wonders of the area, including its insects, plants, and birds.

ACCOMMODATION IN THE OKAVANGO Private tented camps are the only option in the Okavango. The camps are generally small, 8 to 24 beds, and are far from one another, which makes for a low density of safari vehicles when you're game viewing. Trips are generally either high-end, based at luxury tented camps, or low-end camping trips on which you're expected to pitch your tent and help with camp chores.

The Okavango tent lodge is the model for most lodges throughout Southern Africa. Each lodge has between 4 and 10 safari tents, each the size of a modest home bedroom and equipped with two beds, bedroom furniture, and en-suite bathroom. At their priciest, they can be chic and comfortable. A central area with a space for dining, a bar, and a lounge is built on a wooden deck with a thatched roof and walls open to the elements. Dining is often under the stars at a specially laid table.

Malawi

Landlocked Malawi, south of the equator, calls itself the "warm heart of Africa," and in many ways this pocket-size country is just that. Yet it's unlikely to be your first choice for a safari because its parks are relatively small and the game less abundant than elsewhere. The safari industry is fledgling at best, with several game reserves but only one really viable national park—Liwonde. As a result, Malawi attracts people looking for a general African vacation much more than those specifically seeking a big-game safari.

Malawi is one of the poorest nations in Africa despite being, along with Botswana, one of the continent's most peaceful destinations. It's dominated by Lake Malawi, dubbed the "lake of stars" by early travelers. A stay at the lake is a mesmerizing, unforgettable experience. Baobab trees surround the shores, fish eagles call every morning, and nature seems to play its most sublime games with color and clouds each day. The third largest of Africa's Rift Valley lakes, Lake Malawi is the second-longest lake in the world (after Lake Tanganyika) and the third deepest. Its ecology—particularly its variety of cichlid fishes, indigenous river fish that evolved in isolation from a common ancestor 10 million years ago—is one of the continent's natural wonders. Other than fish out of this lake and coffee and tobacco farms that are controlled mainly by expatriate families, Malawi doesn't have many resources.

WHEN TO GO May through October tend to be dry and therefore are best for viewing game. Rain is sporadic the rest of the year; most falls December through March, with afternoon thunderstorms common December through February. November and April experience a similar amount of rainfall; November is better for viewing game, however, because it comes on the heels of the dry season, when grass and bush cover are still relatively thin.

Lake Malawi is a high-risk area for malaria year-round; in the rest of the country, the risk peaks during the wet months, November through April.

Liwonde National Park

The highlight of Liwonde is the Shire River; most of the park is situated on its eastern bank. It's an area of floodplain grasslands, reed swamps, and floating meadows that give refuge to hippopotamuses, crocodiles, and waterbucks, as well as an abundance of elephants and swampland birds. Within the park are also lions, leopards, warthogs, and various antelope species, including the rare suni, also known as Livingstone's antelope. You can go game viewing in open vehicles and small motorboats, walking with a guide, or on bicycle trips to visit local villages. You can also do a three-day camping trip on the park's hiking trail.

ACCOMMODATION IN LIWONDE The only accommodation in Liwonde is Wilderness Safaris' private luxury Mvuu Wilderness Lodge, a beautiful camp with five tents overlooking the Shire River. Wilderness also runs neighboring Mvuu Camp, which is used for mobile safaris.

Namibia

A vast wedge of land bounded by the icy Atlantic on the west, the Kalahari Desert on the east, the Kunene River on the north, and the Orange River on the south, this elemental place, dubbed "the land that God made in anger," is arguably the most beguiling area of Southern Africa. The people attracted to it invariably develop an almost obsessive passion about it. Like any other arid place, Namibia is full of natural wonders. Foremost among these, in addition to the Namib Desert and the vast, shallow depression known as the Etosha Pan, is the Fish River Canyon, second in size only to the Grand Canyon.

The Namib, one of the world's oldest and driest deserts, runs along the western coast, also known as the Skeleton Coast for its stark yet beautiful, towering sand-and-granite walls. Inland, an escarpment runs the length of the country and separates the desert from the savanna to the east. Etosha National Park, located in the semi-arid region between desert and grasslands, consists mainly of salt pans that stretch to the horizon and beyond and is the remnant of an inland sea that lay in the geological past. Both the desert and the plains are game country; some of the best safaris are into the Skeleton Coast, where you encounter elephants as well as the pre-industrial Himba people, one of several cultures in Africa that seem to exist oblivious to the pace and tools of modern life.

German colonists tamed awesome territory when they colonized this country. It can take a whole day just to get from one settlement to the next—sometimes these places are just a fuel stop and trading store. The capital, Windhoek, is small but modern, with remnants of its Germanic past; Swakopmund, a coastal town, is like a living museum of late-19th-century colonial architecture and German culture.

WHEN TO GO The best time to travel to Namibia is winter, May through October. Rain usually falls in summer, with a short rainy season in November and the main rainy season from February to March, which is also prime malaria season. In the Namib Desert, rain sometimes doesn't fall for 10 years or more. Summers are hot, winter days warm to hot, and winter nights cold to downright freezing.

Etosha National Park

Etosha, which translates as "the great white place," consists of 13,830 square mi of saline desert, savanna, and woodlands. Classified as a saline desert, the expansive terrain here changes from densely wooded thickets to wide-open spaces and from white salt-encrusted pans to blond grasslands; it's an unusual setting for game. What sets Etosha apart from other reserves in Africa is the 3,800-square-mi Etosha Pan. On some days the pan is a shimmering sheet of mirages on which animals appear to be floating on air. Of the 114 mammal species represented in the park, several—such as the black rhinoceros and the black-faced impala—are rare and endangered. Game drives are the main activity inside the national park. Many visitors drive their own vehicles into the park.

ACCOMMODATION IN ETOSHA Etosha was developed while Namibia was governed by South Africa, so its three national parks camps (known here as rest camps)—Namutoni, Okaukuejo, and Halali—feel like those in South Africa. These parks offer camping as well as lodging in bungalows, except for Namutoni, which is a German frontier fort and has rooms in the old fort building. Geared to the local market, prices are very reasonable for foreign travelers. Outside Namutoni gate are three large, mid- to high-priced lodges with bungalow rooms, as well as Wilderness Safaris' luxury Ongava Lodge within a private area bordering the park.

Skeleton Coast National Park

The best way to see this driest of all African places is to fly in by small charter plane to one of the private concessions. You can also visit via mobile safari, or by renting a 4×4, driving yourself and staying at public rest camps—although only one of these, Sossusvlei in the south, has any camping facilities, and they are basic. In the north, the famed and mysterious Kaokoland is home to nomadic Himba pastoralists as well as Namibia's amazing desert elephants. You may also be able to see desert black rhinoceroses. There are also vast seal colonies along the coast, and although the desert life you see in the dunes and gravel here might not be what springs to mind when you imagine a safari, it is unique and precious. Nature drives here explore the region's fascinating geology and landscapes and search for rare desert species, including desert elephants, brown hyena, and Hartman's zebra.

ACCOMMODATION IN SKELETON COAST The only accommodations are on a few private safari concessions, most notably Wilderness Safaris' Skeleton Coast Lodge, a tent camp created to have a minimal impact on the desert both visually and ecologically. All walkways are on raised platforms above the sand of a dry river floodplain, all water is trucked in, and all garbage is flown out. Power is solar-provided, and no laundry is done at the camp. (Linens and laundry are flown to Windhoek to be washed.)

South Africa

South Africa has one of the proudest and longest conservation records in the world. What characterizes most of the 17 national parks and many provincial reserves in South Africa from those in the rest of Southern Africa is pretty much what separates the country from its neighbors: the parks are highly organized and tightly managed by conservation authorities under rigorous scientific scrutiny. The parks also have good roads, plentiful and cheap accommodations, and excellent facilities. The crown jewel of South Africa's reserves is Kruger National Park, the second-largest game reserve in Africa, which has its origins in conservation legislation from 1889. Kruger, a magnificent wilderness that is home to an astonishing number of animals, is completely open to the public, like all of South Africa's parks, and you can tour and view game from the comfort of your car. Kruger is also at the core of Limpopo Transfrontier Park, the largest conservation area in the world, consisting of about 2 million square km (800,000 square mi).

South Africa's exclusive (and pricey) private game lodges provide wildlife experiences without parallel. You could spend a month bumping fenders with tourist minibuses in East Africa and never get as close to game as in these lodges. Bouncing over dirt tracks in an open Land Rover, you *know* you're in Africa. These luxury lodges give you a taste of the bush and the experience of living out in the wilds, and nothing stops an elephant from joining you for dinner. But you get comfortable beds, flush toilets, running water, hot showers—even air-conditioning.

First-time visitors to South Africa are often surprised to find cities full of skyscrapers, multilane highways, and just about all the conveniences and modern infrastructure of home. It's true that the country still has large ghetto townships outside major cities as well as vast rural areas where people live at subsistence levels; but as the country has developed economically since the end of apartheid, more money and jobs, often based on tourism, are trickling down to the parts of the population that need them. Originally a Dutch then a British colony, the country fought a bitter civil war in the late 1800s before gaining independence. Nearly 50 years of apartheid rule followed until democracy arrived in 1994 with Nelson Mandela as the new regime's first president. Today, although still battling a sluggish economy and high unemployment, this fledgling democracy is forging ahead with new initiatives to improve its global position and in doing so is providing a cautiously optimistic outlook for the future.

WHEN TO GO Summer—that is, November through February—is high season in South Africa because that's when South Africans take their vacations. However, the weather can be hot, with temperatures frequently reaching 100°F in January and February. Winters are mild and traditionally the best time for viewing game. Keep in mind though that in July temperatures in Kruger can dip down to the freezing point, and in the Kalahari temperatures can drop to 10°F. In Zululand temperatures seldom rise above the mid-80s, but it can get very humid; on the other hand, winters are warm and seldom cold. In Kruger, the Kalahari, and Zululand, the annual rains fall from late November through February, mostly in the form of afternoon thundershowers. The remainder of the year is predominantly dry and, as there are no mass migrations, the game viewing is good almost year-round. The winter months, July and August, are perceived to be low season, and therefore, fewer tourists frequent the private lodges. In fact, this is a superb time for game viewing and you can find some great deals.

In many safari locations, including Kruger, summer is the high malaria season. Malaria is not a problem in urban areas of South Africa, the provinces around Cape Town, and the Kalahari.

Hluhluwe-Umfolozi Park

In lush Zululand is Hluhluwe-Umfolozi (pronounced Shloo-*shloo*-ee Uhm-fuh-*loe*-zee), a reserve with one of the most biologically diverse habitats on the planet—a unique mix of forest, woodland, savanna, and grassland with about 1,250 species of plants and trees. It's best known for saving the white rhinoceros from extinction, and a visit to this park should produce great sightings of rhinoceroses, among other animals, including the rest of the Big Five. The park is run by the provincial Ezemvelo KwaZulu-Natal Wildlife (Ezemvelo is Zulu for "environment").

Compared with Kruger, Hluhluwe-Umfolozi is tiny—less than 6% of Kruger's size—but such comparisons can be misleading. You can spend days driving around this park and still not see everything, or feel like you're going in circles. The biggest advantage Hluhluwe has over Kruger is that game viewing is good year-round, whereas Kruger has seasonal peaks and valleys. Another bonus is its proximity to Greater St. Lucia Wetland Park (a World Heritage site), which has inexpensive boat trips and guided walks, which generally last two to three hours, to see hippopotamuses and crocodiles up close as well as many species of birds. Experienced rangers can lead you on wilderness trails over a period of days if you reserve well in advance and feel comfortable walking 10 mi of relatively rugged terrain a day. These trails are one of the finest wilderness experiences you can get in Africa for less than US$100 a person a day all-inclusive.

Most visitors see the park from their own cars—private vehicles are allowed in the park from sunrise to sunset. Consider joining a ranger-led game drive, though, which has several advantages over self-driving. You sit in a high seat in an open vehicle for the best possible views. The ranger can explain the finer points of animal behavior and local ecology; he also knows the best spots to find leopards, cheetahs, lions, and other animals. Drives are offered in the morning and at night.

ACCOMMODATION IN HLUHLUWE-UMFOLOZI As in the national parks, accommodation is in huts and chalets that are inexpensive and fully equipped but fairly basic. Unfortunately, most of the park's secluded bush lodges and camps must be reserved in a block, and as the smallest houses at least eight people, only groups can use them. This leaves the more modern, and quite comfortable, Hilltop Camp, which accepts nongroup reservations. It has thatch-roof chalets with private bathrooms and small verandas or small, basic rondavels with shared bathroom facilities. At this writing, private lodges are in the works.

Imagine yourself bathed in sunlight, wind whipping through your hair and no cell phones, no e-mail, no **TRAVEL LOG** television or radio—just the wondrous animals, knowledgeable rangers, and, of course, South Africa in all its splendid beauty. And then there are the surprises. As if spotting giraffes, elephants, and buffalo weren't enough, imagine the excitement of stumbling upon several lions devouring the remains of an impala. Disgusted, yet at the same time strangely engrossed, I was unable to look away, sitting in silence for almost an hour, captivated by the sight of predators feeding on their prey.

–Stephanie K., New York, NY

Kgalagadi Transfrontier Park

In an odd finger of South Africa, jutting north and surrounded by Botswana in the east and Namibia in the west, is the giant Kgalagadi Transfrontier Park, South Africa's second-largest park after Kruger National Park. Kgalagadi was officially launched in 2000 as the first transfrontier, or "peace park," in Southern Africa by merging South Africa's vast Kalahari Gemsbok National Park with the even larger Gemsbok National Park in Botswana.

The Kgalagadi Transfrontier is less commercialized and less developed than Kruger. Due to the absence of surface water for most of the year in this vast desert, some of the bigger game species, such as elephants and rhinoceroses, are absent—but because there's less vegetation, the animals that are here are much more visible. The landscape—endless red sand dunes punctuated with blond grass and the odd thorn tree—is dominated by two dry riverbeds, where most of the game and large carnivores are concentrated: the Nossob (which forms the border between South Africa and Botswana), and its tributary, the Auob. The Nossob flows only a few times a century, and the Auob flows only once every few decades or so. A single road runs beside each riverbed. Along these roads windmills pump water into man-made water holes that help the animals survive and provide unsurpassed viewing and photo opportunities for visitors. A third road traverses the park's interior to join the other two. Allow a full day for the long and dusty drive, which is 124 km (77 mi) one-way.

The park is famous for its gemsbok (also known as oryx), its large black-mane lions, and a host of rare desert species such as the springbok, the elusive aardvark, and the tiny Cape fox. Another highlight is one of Africa's greatest concentrations of raptors, including Bateleur eagles, lappet-faced vultures, pygmy falcons, and the cooperatively hunting red-necked falcons and gabar goshawks. Joining these are leopards, cheetahs, eland, blue wildebeests, meerkats, and mongooses.

The key to appreciating this barren place is to understand how its creatures have adapted to their harsh surroundings for survival. The gemsbok, for example, can tolerate extreme changes in body temperature. The white area around the animal's nose is home to a sophisticated cooling system that lowers the blood temperature before it circulates to the head. There are insects in the park that inhale only every half hour or so to conserve the moisture that breathing expends.

You can see most of the park by driving yourself in an ordinary car or by taking a 4×4 on specially marked trails. However, you shouldn't miss the park's legendary night drives, which depart every evening from Twee Rivieren Camp. Reservations are essential and can be made when you book your accommodations. The drives go out just as the park gate closes to everyone else. Your vantage point is from an open truck high off the ground that seats about 30; a ranger gives a brief background on the history, animals, plants, and insects of the Kalahari before setting off. By spotlight you have a chance to pick out rare nocturnal animals like the brown hyena and the bat-eared fox.

ACCOMMODATION IN KGALAGADI There are three rest camps in the park—Twee Rivieren (named for the two rivers that join here), Nossob, and Mata Mata. Twee Rivieren is the most modern, has the best shop for food supplies, and is the only camp with a restaurant. All three camps have bungalows or cottages that sleep up to six, so they're an even better value if you're traveling with your family or large party. Accommodations have a fully equipped kitchen, a *braai* (barbecue), and bathroom facilities.

Three small wilderness camps in the park offer exclusive accommodation and an experience as close as you can get to the African wilderness without camping yourself.

Kruger National Park

Unlike many other Southern African and all East African reserves, the public area of Kruger National Park is a destination most people see from their own cars. Although game drives with private companies are available from some of the larger rest camps, and most rest camps offer guided night drives, the park is full of private vehicles. Concessions around the park's borders contain private lodges.

Here, you're allowed to drive yourself in your own car—called self-driving—between sunrise and sunset. You need to reserve well in advance for multiday overnight hikes, led by an armed ranger and involving either backpacking or using rudimentary trail huts.

The Kruger Park is chockablock with the Big Five—lions, leopards, elephants, buffalo, and rhinoceroses—but leopards are hard to find in their riverine habitat and rhinoceroses are common only in the southwest corner (near the Berg en Dal and Pretoriuskop rest camps). Other predators, such as wild dogs, are here, too, but are skittish and hard to spot. Lions, buffalo, and especially elephants can be seen anywhere. Plains game—giraffes, zebras, wildebeests or gnus, and antelope—are ubiquitous, as are birds of prey. Consult the game-viewing book in each rest camp to find out where game is being seen. It's also a custom in South Africa to stop other cars and ask their passengers what they've spotted.

ACCOMMODATION IN KRUGER Several larger rest camps have laundry facilities and pools, and some even have open-air cinemas, where wildlife documentaries are shown in the evening. In the public rest camps, a day in the park costs about US$38 to US$50 (R250 to R330) per person, including meals.

Seven private concessions within Kruger have accommodations that are modeled on private lodges, with elegant rooms, handsome furnishings, and lots of personal attention from staff and rangers. Kruger is big enough that rest-camp and private-lodge guests don't run into each other. The Hamilton's and Jock private-style game lodges, which charge between US$180 and US$330 per person a night, are the most notable of the options. Jock's 12 opulent bungalows are at the confluence of two rivers, an ideal site for game spotting. Hamilton's six tents have private verandas and butler service. The lodge has both bush walks and game drives.

PRIVATE GAME RESERVES AROUND KRUGER

Many luxury private lodges are outside the western boundary of Kruger National Park, and most form part of the adjacent Greater Kruger National Park. These outlying areas are split into four private game reserves: the Sabi Sand, Thornybush, Timbivati, and Manyaleti. The Sabi Sand has some 20 private lodges, including the ultraluxurious Singita and Sabi Sabi, CC Africa's Londolozi, classic Mala Mala, and smaller, less-expensive Lion Sands. The Sabi Sand has the most consistent game sightings in South Africa: on a two-night, three-day stay in the area you should see at least the Big Five and much, much more. Private lodges stake their reputations on their personal service and attention to detail; costs range from US$250 per person a day to as much as US$1,000 per person a day. Lodge styles are almost universally chic African ethnic and standards are top-notch. All activities are included, as are meals, which are often on par with those served in fine restaurants; most alcoholic and other beverages and often laundry services are included as well.

Tswalu Kalahari Reserve

At 563 square mi, Tswalu, near Kgalagadi Transfrontier Park, is the biggest privately owned game reserve in Africa. It spreads over endless Kalahari dunes and over much of the Korannaberg Mountain range. It's the best place in Africa to see rhinoceroses—the reserve has more than 50 white and 11 black rhinos, which have adapted to the desert. Other rare species here include roan and sable antelope, black wildebeests, and mountain zebras. The sparse vegetation makes for spectacular sightings, and because there are only three or so Land Rovers traversing the entire area, you feel as though you have the entire desert to yourself.

ACCOMMODATION IN TSWALU Tswalu, a Relais & Châteaux property, has two luxury lodgings that together can accommodate a maximum of 34 guests. At Motse, near the center of the reserve, nine freestanding thatch-and-stone suites cluster around the large main building. A heated pool looks out onto grasslands, and a sundeck overlooks a water hole. Tarkuni, in its own section of the reserve, sleeps 8 to 12 and has four main bedrooms with en-suite bathrooms, its own chef, Land Rover, and tracker, and a heated pool.

Zambia

Zambia has 19 national parks and 31 adjacent game-management areas, but of these, only a few receive regular visitors. Although some of the reserves are protected in little more than name alone, it's still an impressive conservation record for a relatively poor and underdeveloped nation. Zambia is in many ways like Botswana was 20 years ago, before modern tourism took off and big safari companies homogenized the business. The land is extremely remote and a tourism infrastructure is almost nonexistent. Therefore, Zambia isn't recommended for first-time visitors. However, if you want adventure, Zambia is sublime and the challenges involved in getting there make it all the more attractive.

Although Zambia's interior is composed of seemingly endless arid savanna, its borders are defined by water: the mighty Zambezi in the southwest, with Victoria Falls (known as Mosi-oa-Tunya here) at its center; lakes Mweru and Bangweulu and the Laupula River in the northwest; the east, cut by the Luangwa River, the southern extremity of the Great Rift Valley; and Lake Tanganyika, the world's longest and second-deepest freshwater reservoir, to the north. The main safari destinations in Zambia include the South and North Luangwa national parks and Kafue National Park, Zambia's largest game reserve.

South Luangwa is the most popular safari destination, with several small lodges run by sophisticated but bush-wise expatriate families. North Luangwa National Park is as wild a place as exists in Africa, currently with only two, dry-season reed-and-thatch camps that are washed away by floods every November and reconstructed when the dry season sets in, around June or July. American conservationists Mark and Delia Owens helped to put North Luangwa on the map with their daring anti-poaching work here in the late 1980s and early 1990s. Kafue is likewise mostly undeveloped.

Zambia may strike you as a time capsule of the safari era between the two World Wars. Traces of British tradition remain—tinkling glasses of G&T at sundowner time, pith helmets, the occasional plummy accent. The veneer is British, but realize that most of the whites here were born in Zambia and are very bush savvy; they can tell lion from leopard spoor at a glance.

WHEN TO GO Winter, June through October, is best for game viewing as seasonal water sources dry up and game teems around the main waterways. However, this time of year is dusty, and nights can be bitterly cold. April, May, November, and December, although considered the "green season" because of rain, may still offer reasonable viewing. The best time for birding is during the summer migration, from November to April. This is also the time of torrential rains, heat, and mosquitoes; some of the best game-viewing areas, such as North Luangwa National Park, become inaccessible. The threat of malaria is high from November to May.

Kafue National Park

Zambia's largest park, Kafue, is 150 mi west of the capital, Lusaka, yet feels much more remote than South Luangwa National Park, which is twice as far away from the capital. This is partly because of the extremely limited access to the park in the summer rainy season; due to the rains, most safari camps close for four or five months a year. Kafue stretches over 13,970 square mi, with large wetlands, or *dambos,* in the south, and the Serengeti-like Busanga Plains in the north. Large herds of elephants and antelope and more than 400 bird species make the park their home. In the south are semi-aquatic antelope such as lechwe, puku, and Defassa waterbuck; in the northern miombo woodlands are large sable and roan antelope. Bird-watching throughout the park is superb. The best way to see game here is in open-vehicle drives and walking with a guide.

ACCOMMODATION IN KAFUE Overland safari operators set up their own "fly camps"—groups of small tents set up in a new location at the end of each day—in the choice spots where public campsites have either been destroyed or allowed to disintegrate. Private lodges are mostly timber constructions or tented camps, catering to those who don't need much more than the basic necessities of plain food, a bucket shower, and a good drink at the end of the day.

South Luangwa National Park

The Luangwa Valley, which marks the end of the Great Rift Valley, is one of the last unspoiled wilderness areas and possibly one of the finest wildlife sanctuaries in Africa. It covers nearly 6,600 square mi and is crossed by the meandering Luangwa River, a large south-flowing tributary of the east–west Zambezi. The valley's lagoons, woodlands, and plains host huge concentrations of game, including elephants, buffalo, lions, giraffes, and hippopotamuses. Leopards are more plentiful in South Luangwa than in any other Southern African game park, and your chances of seeing them are almost guaranteed. Game viewing here includes canoe trips, drives in open vehicles, or, the most popular option, guided multiday walking trips in areas not accessible to vehicles. The superb Robin Pope Safaris was the first to undertake this type of walking safari in Zambia, and Pope has gained the reputation as the best in the field.

ACCOMMODATION IN SOUTH LUANGWA An all-weather road, one of the few in any park in Zambia, starts at the Mfuwe Gate entrance to South Luangwa National Park, and as a result there are several permanent lodges near here. The farther away you get from this paved road, the more difficult transportation becomes during the rainy summer season, and the longer the camps have to remain closed during this period. At the farthest northern point in the park, many camps are so remote that they're reached by boat even in winter, and in summer they close entirely. The most exciting option for accommodations in South Luangwa is at a private tented camp such as Robin Pope's Tena Tena. These large tents usually have reed walls and private bathrooms.

Zimbabwe

With its unspoiled wilderness and outstanding variety of wildlife, Zimbabwe is an exceptional destination for seeing game. Many endangered species that once roamed a good part of the continent can still be found in the reserves here. The country's poor governance and the resulting bad press obscure the fact that Zimbabwe has one of the longest and proudest conservation records in Africa, as well as some of the finest national parks. The main parks—Hwange, Matusadona, and Mana Pools—have excellent public and private facilities and an infrastructure that is, for the most part, well serviced. It's true, however, that since Zimbabwe's independence, game conservation has been low on the government's list of priorities; the land seized by supporters of President Robert Mugabe in 2001 and 2002 included farms and also many game reserves and private game ranches. Recent years have seen increased poaching in some national parks. Still, the main parks remain good safari destinations that maintain a strong sense of wild Africa. Zimbabwe is the only country in Africa with an association for professional guides and hunters; its guides have to pass the most rigorous tracking and bush-craft tests in Africa.

Hwange National Park, in the northwest corner of the country, abuts the Kalahari basin and is famous for its elephant herds. Not far north is Victoria Falls, one of the world's great natural wonders and the core of a safari area bordering the western arm of the Zambezi River. If you head east along the mighty Zambezi, you come to Lake Kariba and Matusadona National Park. Mana Pools National Park, on the lower Zambezi River in the country's remote northern reaches, is a top spot for safaris, especially walking safaris.

At this writing, political violence, economic instability, and other developments are troubling the country. The tourism industry has been surprisingly resilient, and there appears to be little to no threat to visitors in the main tourist areas. The healthy air-charter industry allows for easy access from one safari destination to another. Driving yourself anywhere in the country is not recommended. When planning a Zimbabwean safari, check with the U.S. Department of State for the latest travel advisories and warnings.

WHEN TO GO Winter, about March through October, is predominantly dry, with cool temperatures and good game viewing. The peak season, July through October, is also when malarial risk is at a low. The annual rains fall in summer, from late November through February, mostly in the form of afternoon thundershowers; vegetation is dense and tall during this time, hindering game spotting. Summer temperatures can soar above 100°F in the low-lying Zambezi Valley. Canoe safaris on the Zambezi River are run most of the year and are most popular from April to November.

Hwange National Park

Zimbabwe's premier wildlife park, Hwange is best known for its large elephant population (almost 40,000 at last count); sightings of lions, leopards, wild dogs, and cheetahs, as well as of the smaller African wild cat, serval, honey badger, nocturnal civet, and hyena, are also excellent here. The park's ecological diversity—from vast palm-fringed plains to grasslands, acacia woodlands to mopane forests—ensures continued food supply throughout the year for buffalo, sable and roan antelope, giraffes, wildebeests, impalas, gemsboks, and dozens of other animals.

Multiday wilderness trails led by experienced rangers need to be reserved well in advance. Day and night game drives in open vehicles are offered.

ACCOMMODATION IN HWANGE Accommodation here includes rondavels, huts, and chalets that are all fairly inexpensive and fully equipped for self-catering. Although quite basic, the accommodations are comfortable and cost a fraction of what you would pay at a private lodge. Private concession areas in and on the outskirts of Hwange do offer small luxury camps, including Makalolo Plains, Linkwasha, and Giraffe Springs (all run by Wilderness Safaris). These tented accommodations are in the southern sector; there's also a well-regarded lodge on the park's unfenced eastern border, run by Touch the Wild.

Lake Kariba & Matusadona National Park

When constructed in 1958, Lake Kariba was the largest man-made lake in the world. After the valley was flooded, the tops of mopane and other trees remained above the water where they stand today like fossilized relics from an earlier age, providing perches for cormorants, kingfishers, and fish eagles. The black skeletal branches of these ghostly trees form an indelible image, particularly when framed against a molten sunset. Elephants and buffalo swarm the banks, and the waters of the lake support more than 40 species of fish as well as crocodiles and hippopotamuses. Matusadona National Park fronts the south side of the lake and offers excellent game viewing from boats, canoes, and open vehicles, as well as on guided walks. The area is one of few where black rhinos can be seen regularly; they were reintroduced in the 1990s after being poached almost into extinction during the previous decade.

ACCOMMODATION IN MATUSADONA Along the shores of Lake Kariba are a dozen or so private lodges that range in price and style. The lodging highlight here is Wilderness Safaris' luxury camp, Matusadona Water Wilderness, where you stay in floating chalets and travel between your room and common areas by motorized pontoon or canoe. There are also small public campgrounds with communal cooking areas and public bathrooms (known throughout Africa as ablution blocks).

Mana Pools National Park

Mana Pools is the main game park of "the Valley" (as the lower Zambezi River Valley is known), one of Africa's oldest and greatest safari areas. It is renowned for the large number of elephants, buffalo, hippopotamuses, crocodiles, and eland that congregate along the lush green river banks in winter, particularly September and October. Lions and leopards are numerous if less easily seen. Birdlife at Mana is also sensational, with more than 380 species recorded. Among them are the brilliant carmine bee-eaters, Lilian's lovebirds, hornbills, leggy saddle-billed storks, ibis, jacanas, orioles, herons, and Bateleur eagles.

ACCOMMODATION IN MANA POOLS The best way to see Mana Pools is either on an inexpensive multiday camping and canoeing trip on the Zambezi River, offered April through November by Natureways and other outfitters, or by staying at one of the two intimate luxury lodges run by Wilderness Safaris—Chikwenya, with thatch-roof tented rooms, and chalet-based Ruckomechi, set under massive acacias. The park offers wilderness campsites from May to September, but these are recommended for those who are truly bush savvy.

EAST AFRICA

Safaris in East Africa were popularized a century ago by big-game hunters such as Frederick Selous and Theodore Roosevelt. Images of the wide-open plains of the Serengeti, covered from horizon to horizon with animals, stuck in our collective consciousness. Not all of East Africa is quite like this. The region encompasses forests, mountains, and arid desert areas—all with plenty of animals if not in quite the same numbers as seen on the Serengeti. For many, East Africa is also synonymous with safari romance, conjured up by the likes of Karen Blixen (a.k.a. Isak Dinesen) in her classic *Out of Africa,* and developed further by Ernest Hemingway, Robert Ruark, and Elspeth Huxley. James Fox chronicled the tales of intrigue and infidelity among the wealthy, polo-playing British expatriates of "Happy Valley," in the Abedare highlands north of Nairobi.

The safari industry boomed in East Africa in the 1970s. It was then that hotel-size lodges were built and closed minibuses were introduced to move large numbers of visitors around the busiest parks. This safari style was conceived of as a safety precaution (which it continues to be), but many in the industry think these precautions are unnecessary.

Kenya

National parks and reserves occupy almost 10% of Kenya. Amboseli National Park might offer the classic picture of Kenya—elephants grazing on lush grasses, snowcapped Kilimanjaro rising beyond in neighboring Tanzania—but it's the Masai Mara reserve, a northerly extension of the Serengeti ecosystem, that has Kenya's greatest wildlife. The greater Serengeti is also a backdrop for the annual wildebeest migration, when more than a million of these gentle creatures, accompanied by tens of thousands of zebras as well as other herbivores, arrive en masse from Tanzania's Serengeti in search of grass. Nevertheless, purists argue that Kenya has even better places for safari, including Tsavo, Samburu, and Meru. They also point to the Great Rift Valley lakes and reserves, such as Lake Bagoria, where tens of thousands of flamingos congregate, as well as Naivasha and the legendary Lake Turkana, a sprawling desert miracle often referred to as the Jade Sea.

Although plagued by decades of corrupt one-party autocracy and a severely crippled economy, Kenya took a leap into democracy in late 2002, electing former opposition leader Mwai Kibaki as president. Urban crime is a fact of life here, especially in Nairobi, but safari areas see considerably less criminal activity, which, at worst, runs to petty theft.

Nevertheless, at this writing, the U.S. Department of State is urging Americans to put off nonessential travel to Kenya. In a September 2003 travel warning, it says it continues to see signs of terrorist threats aimed at U.S. and Western interests in the country, with increased risks in Nairobi and the coastal region. When planning a safari in Kenya, check with the State Department for the latest travel advisories and warnings.

WHEN TO GO Game viewing is at its best during the dry months, July through October and January through March. The wildebeests usually start migrating into Kenya in July. On their way to Masai Mara, where they graze through November or so, the herds must traverse the Mara River; the crossing is viewed as a main event, but anticipating its exact timing is difficult, especially when scheduling a visit months in advance.

Kenya has two rainy seasons, when malaria risk is highest: the long, or big, rains fall in April, May, and part of June, and the short, or small, rains occur in November and part of December. During the period of short rains, there's usually a brief daily shower followed by sunshine. This is an excellent time to go on safari because the crowds are thin, the foliage is deep green, and the murky skies often make for dramatic photographs.

Amboseli National Park

Although it's the smallest game park in the country, Amboseli attracts more visitors than any other reserve in Kenya, after Masai Mara. At the center of the park is a marsh, Engongo Narok (meaning "black and benevolent" in Masai), which swells to a seasonal lake thanks to melting snow that trickles down from Mt. Kilimanjaro, just over the border in Tanzania. This water grants verdant life to the notoriously dusty landscape that dominates the rest of the area.

The view of white-capped Kilimanjaro—a classic image—is a highlight here, but what makes Amboseli so spectacular is the abundance of game: lions, leopards, black rhinos, huge elephant and buffalo herds, and 13 species of antelope. Among the 420 species of birds here is the Taveta golden weaver, which is found nowhere else in the world.

Not even a quarter of the size of the Masai Mara, Amboseli has difficulty managing the crowds it attracts; in July and August, the busiest months, you have to share predator sightings with numerous game-viewing minivans.

ACCOMMODATION IN AMBOSELI Accommodations are largely in lodges, really hotels, that contain about a hundred rooms. Most of these lodges try to compensate for the lack of intimacy by paying a lot of attention to decor, adorning rooms and public areas with African accents and furnishings. Some have watering-hole or Kilimanjaro views. There are a few luxury tented camps, and the national park has simple *banda* (East African huts) and campgrounds.

Not only does your body feel alive on safari, but your mind does, too. You are constantly learning from local

TRAVEL LOG

Kenyans, experts in their fields, eager to share their knowledge and culture. Every plant and tree has a story, and even many of the animals seem to have an opinion. After lunch, as we sipped our Kenyan coffee overlooking the Uaso Nyiro River, Peter, our guide, up-dated us on the current political climate. The hippos partially submerged in the river below seemed to be from an opposing party and let their views be known with a deep chorus of "wa-ha-ha-ha-haaa" whenever Peter paused. "A man without culture is like a zebra without stripes" was the constant refrain of our Masai driver, William. Despite his khaki uniform and impec-cable English, he upheld his tribe's way of life: proud of his heritage and customs, he spoke in full Masai dress after dinner at the Mara Safari Club, illuminat-ing us with his understanding of both worlds.

–Alice R., New York City

Masai Mara National Reserve

The best-known reserve in Kenya, the Masai Mara is a land of undulating hills and rolling grasslands. It has the largest population of lions in Africa; elephants, cheetahs, leopards, African buffalo (also known as Cape buffalo), giraffes, gazelles, hippos, and topi antelope are also abundant. Hundreds of hippos and crocodiles, including some of Africa's largest, inhabit the Mara River.

Game drives in a minibus with an open roof hatch are the main activity. Most lodges also offer early-morning hot-air-balloon rides, and small companies lead walks or horseback rides across the Aitong Plains and Loita Hills. Because each lodge in the reserve accommodates nearly 200 people, overcrowding can be an issue during peak season. The crowds are thickest when the massive wildebeest migration reaches (around July) the opposite side of the Mara River's main ford, where giant crocodiles await a veritable buffet of plains animals.

Although rainy at times, the low season can provide excellent game viewing at very reasonable rates and without the crowds—but also without the spectacle of the migration.

ACCOMMODATION IN MASAI MARA Several companies run luxury tented safari lodges, which may have anywhere from 4 to 40 tents. Among these are CC Africa's secluded Bateleur Camp and the intimate Cottar's 1920s Camp, in a private 22,000-acre reserve on Masai Mara's fringes. The park also contains hotel-like lodges, several of which have between 80 and 100 rooms. The park's sole campground, next to the warden's office, has basic campsites, ablution blocks, and a few bandas.

Samburu National Reserve

Samburu, the least known of Kenya's main game reserves, lies at the southern edge of the arid region formerly known as the Northern Frontier District but not far from the lush highland farming areas around the base of Mt. Kenya, to the south. The land here is mostly semi-arid plains covered in thornbush; cutting through the landscape is a thick band of rich woodland that runs along the Uaso Nyiro River. The greatest attractions are the endemic, often strange, species in the area: Grevy's zebra, Beisa oryx, gerenuk (long-necked antelope), reticulated giraffe, Somali ostrich, Reiney's gazelle, and vulterine guinea fowl. The Buffalo Springs and Shaba national reserves border Samburu and encompass similar terrain and wildlife.

ACCOMMODATION IN SAMBURU Lodging options here include campsites, banda camps for self-catering, large hotel-style properties, and private lodges ranging from modest to luxurious. The upper-end private lodges are all-inclusive but smaller than comparable accommodations in other game reserves and generally less expensive. At the four-tent Elephant Watch Safari Camp, a unique property just upriver from the Save the Elephants research center, you may study elephant behavior with experts in the field. Avoid lodges that offer "leopard sightings"; taken to setting bait to attract the animals, they are ethically questionable and feel much like a zoo at feeding time.

Tsavo National Park

The largest reserve in Kenya, Tsavo National Park encompasses 8,034 square mi, an area about the size of Wales. With this luxury of space, you often can have the vast landscape to yourself. Tsavo has many small volcanic hills, lots of springs, and a great variety of animals, including elephants that appear red from the soil's settled dust. Established in 1948, Tsavo was split in two a year later to make governing the sprawling reserve more manageable. In theory the two parts are of the same park, but they operate autonomously and have separate headquarters, staff, and entrance fees. Tsavo West has better game in general and more lodges; Tsavo East is much wilder, most of it only recently opened to visitors.

ACCOMMODATION IN TSAVO Most private accommodations in Tsavo are in luxury lodges with anywhere from 4 to 35 tents; a few larger lodges contain hotel-style rooms. Although accommodation in the park's two sections is comparable, top-end lodges in Tsavo East are smaller and more isolated than those in Tsavo West, which is busier. National-park facilities include campsites and self-catering banda camps.

Tanzania

The greatest of all of Africa's safari destinations lies along Tanzania's northern border with Kenya: the Serengeti Plain. The awesome wildebeest migration moves across the plains, and the fiercely independent

Masai people still roam freely here, tending their cattle. The Serengeti consists of several reserves, most notably Serengeti National Park and the Ngorongoro Conservation Area. Ngorongoro, occupying an ancient volcanic crater, is home to large numbers of Africa's big game, including rhinoceroses, which are rare in most other parks. The other choices are the larger, lesser-known reserves of the southern safari circuit: Selous and the much more obscure Ruaha.

A former German colony, Tanzania was ceded to Britain after World War I. Aside from a few small memorials to battles fought about a century ago, virtually no signs of its colonial past remain. The experiment of post-independence African socialism has taken a toll on the country, one of the poorest in the world. Derelict towns and crumbling infrastructure are a fact of life here. Even the capital, the port city of Dar es Salaam, is very run-down. That said, the safari industry runs like clockwork here.

WHEN TO GO Game viewing is best in the dry seasons, July through October and January through March. There are two rainy seasons, during which the risk of malaria is highest: the long rains fall in April, May, and part of June, and the short rains come in November and part of December.

Ngorongoro Conservation Area

With a width of 12 mi, Ngorongoro Crater is one of the largest calderas (volcanic craters) in the world. Circling the crater is tropical forest that once extended much farther down the slopes but diminished as the area's population grew. The crater accounts for just a fraction of the conservation area, which was created to protect the remaining forest as well as the Olduvai Gorge and the rest of the magnificent Crater Highlands. The concentration of wildlife is what draws the crowds to the crater; more than 30,000 animals are thought to make it their home.

On clear days you can stand on the rim of the crater and see the floor 2,000 feet below. From this vantage point elephants resemble ants. The flat, grassy plains are home to abundant numbers of wildebeests, hartebeests, gazelles, and zebras. Ngorongoro Crater is also one of the best places to watch lions stalking their prey. To see the crater, you can go on a game drive in a closed van with a pop-up roof, or explore the rim on foot with a guide.

A visit to Ngorongoro would be incomplete without a trip to the famous Olduvai hominid archaeological fossil site. A small roofed display area exhibits some of the principal finds of the region, including early human-like hominids as well as the bones of long-extinct beasts.

ACCOMMODATION IN NGORONGORO You find several large safari lodges in Ngorongoro. CC Africa's Ngorongoro Crater Lodge stands out above the rest—it's a luxurious haven with suites perched on stilts along the crater rim.

Selous Game Reserve

Encompassing 17,500 square mi, Selous is the world's largest single game reserve. You see few other visitors in this vast land far off the beaten safari path, so your trip is likely to have a true wilderness feeling. The Rufiji River is the park's focal point, especially the 4-mi-long Steigler's Gorge. Only the 12% of the reserve north of the Rufiji is reserved for photographic safaris; the 88% south of the river is limited to hunters. The reserve has great herds of buffalo, a large number of elephants, hundreds of hippos, and many predators, but because there's so much ground for them to cover, you're unlikely to see all the game on a short visit. Free to roam anywhere in the reserve, the animals nevertheless seem more wary here than elsewhere in the country. This wariness also makes them harder to spot.

About half of all the wild dogs in Africa use the Selous reserve as their base; although they travel enormous distances, the wild dogs regularly spend time here, so you have a better-than-average chance of spotting these endangered hunters.

Game viewing in vehicles is available and popular in the reserve, but boat trips along the Rufiji are the most exciting activities here. Walking safaris are also an option at some lodges.

ACCOMMODATION IN SELOUS Many of the dozen or so private lodges here seem to cater to groups with little understanding of (or interest in) wildlife. The luxurious and tasteful Sand Rivers Selous Lodge, on the other hand, devotes itself to the experience of being in such a wild place. Its setting along the Rufiji River is awesome and its game guides are excellent. Walking safaris are a specialty at this eight-room lodge.

Serengeti National Park

The name Serengeti originated from the Masai word *siringet,* referring to boundless or extended plains. Game is easier to see on this open land than just about anywhere else in Africa. Unfortunately, the plains offer little cover for lions, cheetahs, and other predators, which therefore are followed relentlessly by the ubiquitous pop-top minivans. In the granite inselbergs or kopjes (small hills), as well as in the riverine forest, lurks the other big cat of Africa, the leopard. It preys on warthogs and duikers (small antelope) but can take anything up to the size of a small zebra and carry the carcass up into a tree. Elephants are common in the central Seronera Valley, and the Masai giraffe is widespread in the acacia woodlands.

Still, few greater natural spectacles exist on Earth than the wildebeest migration between the Serengeti and Kenya's Masai Mara reserve. The migration is a continuous search for grass, and the herbivores cover more than 1,000 mi in a huge clockwise route each year. By June, after the big rains in the main sections of the Serengeti park, the herds reach Grumeti, an isolated area in the north; they then continue northward into Kenya, fording rivers along the way. The migration amounts to a big feast for the crocodiles that inhabit the Grumeti and Mara rivers. The crocs, some of Africa's biggest, can grow to 18 feet in length on their rich diet of wildebeest.

Walking isn't allowed in the park; game viewing is only by minivan with pop-up tops. Another way to see the wildebeest migration is from above, in a hot-air balloon.

ACCOMMODATION IN SERENGETI The central plains area has several large safari hotels with 65 to 80 rooms each. There is also a handful of luxury lodges with 10 to 18 tents. Good smaller lodges include Grumeti River Camp and Klein's Camp.

Uganda

The primate reserves, primarily the gorilla sanctuaries—places like Bwindi Impenetrable Forest and the chimpanzee refuge on Ngamba Island in Lake Victoria—are Uganda's main attractions. The names alone can conjure up mystery and romance.

When Winston Churchill visited Uganda as a young politician he returned with the message that Uganda was the pearl of Africa and that it would rise as the great success story of the continent. By the late 1960s it was well on its way, until a madman named Idi Amin seized control through a bloody army coup and drove the country over the edge of sanity. These were among the darkest days of modern Africa, and it's only now, decades after "Big Dada" Amin was ousted by the Tanzanian tank corps, that this most fertile of equatorial lands has begun to put aside the depravations of the past; unfortunately, unrest in neighboring Congo, Rwanda, and Burundi haven't helped the process. In 1999, as the tourism industry was on the upswing, the strife between Congo and Rwanda spilled across the border, and Hutu extremists kidnapped and killed some tourists. Although this incident was isolated, and all gorilla areas are now patrolled by soldiers, a considerable blow was dealt to tourism, the country's major economic hope. When planning a trip to Uganda, check with the U.S. Department of State for the latest travel advisories and warnings.

WHEN TO GO Uganda is equatorial and the climate varies little from month to month; temperatures rarely exceed 80°F or drop below 55°F. If you're planning to see gorillas and other forest primates, be aware that the heavy rains fall from March through May and October through November; the forests are in the wettest areas and sometimes become impassable by road or on foot. Malaria is not usually a problem in the high elevations where the gorillas live.

Bwindi Impenetrable Forest National Park

The single most intense encounter with wild animals you are ever likely to experience is an hour with Bwindi's gorillas—mankind's huge yet docile near-ancestors. The gorillas are the main attraction, but chimpanzees and monkeys abound as well. In addition, the park has 120 other species of mammal, 200 types of birds, and 346 varieties of butterfly. The landscape here is dramatic, with steep hills and narrow gorges, myriad streams and waterfalls, and forest that brings to mind Tarzan.

Before you head off to see the gorillas, you need to obtain a permit (about US$275). The easiest way to go about this is to use an African-tour operator to handle the logistics of obtaining the permit and booking a guide. Otherwise, you have to appear at a government office in Uganda exactly three months prior to the date on which you plan to start your gorilla trek.

The park has only a few groups of gorillas, and each group can be visited only once in a 24-hour period. Gorilla-viewing groups are limited to eight people each and are permitted to spend only one hour with the gorillas. The gorillas are constantly on the move, so locating your gorilla group may not be easy. Although your guide may find your group in 15 minutes, there's also a chance that you may have to hike in high altitudes for several hours before your encounter, so it's best to be reasonably fit and healthy. Anyway, if you have a cold or similar illness, you won't be permitted to visit the great apes.

ACCOMMODATION NEAR BWINDI Between the town of Kabale and the park entrance are community-run bandas, simple cottages, three tented safari camps, and the old White Horse Inn. Abercrombie & Kent's Gorilla Forest Camp, on the edge of the Bwindi forest, is the most popular option here, although securing a reservation is almost as difficult as getting a gorilla-viewing permit. Its breathtaking location in the rain forest is as close to a true-life Tarzan setting as exists. The tents are exceptionally large, with twin double beds and two en-suite bathrooms each. Five-day packages start at about US$2,500.

Murchison Falls National Park

The Nile River and the impressive Murchison Falls, an explosion of water from between two rock portals that plummets 141 feet, are the park's main draws. Victorian hunter-explorer Sir Samuel Baker, who named the falls after the then president of Britain's Royal Geographic Society, called them the most interesting thing to happen to the Nile from source to sea.

A trip aboard the *Kiboko* (the name translates as "hippopotamus"), piloted by Frances Oyo Okot, master of this part of the river for nearly 50 years, gives you a close-up look at the falls. Thousands of hippopotamuses and massive crocodiles feed on the stunned fish at the bottom of the cascade. The park is also one of Africa's best birding locations, where you have the opportunity to see the bizarre and rare shoebill stork; a bird-watching boat trip along the nearby Kazinga Channel is a must for any avid or aspiring birder.

Although it's a north–south river, the Nile takes an east–west detour here. Game is scarce on the Nile's south side, but the north side has sizable populations of kob and oribi antelope and Jackson's hartebeest; the last viable herd of Rothchild's giraffe; respectable (and increasing) numbers of elephants and lions; and a small but also growing buffalo population.

Because of increased hostile activity by the anti-government Lord's Resistance Army in the area, the U.S. government, at this writing, recommends against travel to the park. Before scheduling a trip here, check the latest travel advisories and warnings from the U.S. State Department.

ACCOMMODATION IN MURCHISON FALLS Among the comfortable and relatively inexpensive choices here are the rustic log cabins at Rabongo, the modern hotel-like Sarova Paraa Lodge, and the Sambiya Lodge, which is near the Kanyiyo chimpanzee-tracking center above the falls. The Nile Safari Camp has tents set on stilts overlooking the mighty river. Rates in the area start at US$150 all-inclusive per person. Simpler options include the huts at the park headquarters at Paraa.

3

Your Safari Style

After you choose the country or countries where you want to base your safari, you need to decide what type of safari suits you best. You might decide to spend the duration of your trip at a single luxury safari lodge; head off on a fly-in safari, where you stay at two or more bush lodges; take a budget self-drive safari; or venture out on a multiday trip on foot, by canoe, on horseback, or by camel or elephant. Or you can travel with a group on a mobile safari, moving about by land or air, and stay in pitched tents or seasonal camps. There are high- and low-end versions of each option, and there's variety within each category. You can always mix and match your options to create your ideal itinerary.

Repeat visitors to Africa tend to choose smaller safari lodges or camps in one of the less-popular reserves. Or, feeling more confident about being in the bush than on previous trips, they may choose more-adventurous safaris, such as walking or canoeing options. The trade-off is that the game spotting on these types of trips is more random; there are no Big Five guarantees, and every good sighting requires effort.

LUXURY LODGE–BASED SAFARIS

The majority of safari goers base their trips at luxury lodges, which may be made up of stone chalets, thatch-roof huts, rondavels, or large suitelike tents. All have hot-and-cold running water, flush toilets, toiletries, laundry service, electricity, and, in most cases, swimming pools. In South African lodges, rooms also have air-conditioning, telephones, hair dryers, and minibars. The most lavish places also have private plunge pools.

Although a stay at a luxury lodge is the most popular type of safari and offers many exciting moments, it's rather sedentary—you spend a lot of time sitting and eating.

A Day at a Luxury Lodge

You are awakened in the dark—anytime from 5 AM in summer to 7 AM in winter—by a cheerful voice. Within 15 to 30 minutes you're in the dining area, having coffee and a light breakfast with your guide. A half hour to an hour after waking, you climb into a game-drive vehicle and head off in search of animals, which are most active before the heat of the day sets in. The morning drive usually lasts three or four hours. You might see lions feasting on a kill from the previous night or zebras having a breakfast of grass, and you'll stop for coffee as the sun rises. At the end of the drive you return to the lodge for a huge cooked brunch.

Afternoons are for napping, bird-watching around camp, and reading, with time for a dip in the pool if there is one. Some lodges offer a guided game walk or arrange visits to local villages.

In midafternoon you gather in the dining area for high tea. Then it's back into the game-drive vehicle for the evening ride to look for animals waking up from their late-day naps or getting ready for their evening hunting. This ride lasts three to four hours and usually includes a stop at sunset for cocktails, called sundowners. In addition to providing refreshment, these stops allow you to quietly savor—without exhaust fumes and engine noise—the sounds, sights, and smells of this most magical time in the bush. On the slow drive back to camp, a powerful spotlight may be used to illuminate nocturnal animals. After a brief period for freshening up, dinner is served, often in a circular outdoor area called a *boma,* followed by drinks around the campfire, and, if your hosts are amenable, fireside stories. You can turn in whenever you like, but remember that you need to be up before the sun the next day.

TIP You'll be awed by the brilliance of the night skies on safari, especially if you live in a city. To add romance and interest to your stargazing, study up on the southern skies and bring a star guide.

FLY-IN SAFARIS

The mode of transportation for fly-in safaris is as central to the experience as the accommodations. In places such as northern Botswana and southern Tanzania, where few roads are paved, or northern Namibia, where distances make road transfers impractical, small bush planes take you from lodge to lodge. These planes are usually six-seat Cessna 206 craft flown by bush pilots. The planes have no air-conditioning and in summer can be quite warm, especially in the afternoon. If flying in small planes makes you uncomfortable, this type of safari is not for you.

However, flying from destination to destination is a special experience. The planes stay at low altitudes, allowing you to spot game along the way; sometimes you can see, for example, elephant and buffalo herds lined up drinking along the edges of remote water holes or large numbers of zebras walking across the plains. Fly-in safaris also allow you to cover more territory than other types of safaris. In Botswana, for example, the trip between the diverse game destinations of the Moremi Wildlife Reserve and northern Chobe National Park is 40 minutes by plane; it would take six hours by vehicle, if a road between these locations existed.

Hopping from place to place by plane is so easy and fast that many travelers make the mistake of cramming their itineraries with too many lodges. Plan your trip this way and you'll spend more time at airstrips, in planes, and shuttling to and from the airfields than tracking animals or enjoying the bush. You will glimpse animals as you travel back and forth—sometimes you'll even see them on the airstrips—but you won't have time to stop and really take in the sights. If possible, spend at least two nights at any one lodge; three nights is even better.

Lighten Up

The key to fly-in safaris is to pack light. In East Africa, baggage weight on small planes generally cannot exceed 35 pounds per person; in Southern Africa where planes are usually smaller, the maximum allowed is 26 pounds (South Africa is the exception to this rule). Your bag should be a soft-side duffel or something similar, so the pilot can easily fit it into the small cargo area. Consider also that the less you bring the more time you'll save packing and unpacking every time you switch lodges.

TIP If your bag is over the weight limit, or if you weigh more than 220 pounds, you will be required to purchase an additional plane seat (usually about US$100).

WALKING SAFARIS

Many lodges offer walks as an optional way to view game. On a walking safari, however, you spend most, if not all, of your time in the bush on foot, accompanied by an armed guide. Because you're trekking through big-game country, there's an element of danger. But it's the proximity to wilderness that makes this type of trip so enchanting—and exciting. Of course, you can't stop every step of the way or you'd never get very far, but you will stop frequently to be shown something—from a native flower to spoor to animals—or to discuss some aspect of animal behavior or of tracking. Some walking safaris cover more distance than others, and their primary aim is to reach the next checkpoint; others move at a much slower pace, in order to concentrate on gaining bush knowledge and seeing animals and wildlife. They usually last for three days and four nights.

Walking treks take place on what are known as wilderness trails, which are natural tracks made by animals and are traversed only on foot, never by vehicle, to maintain their pristine condition. These trails usually lead into remote areas that you would never see on a typical safari. In most cases, porters or donkeys carry the supplies and bags. Accommodation is usually in remote camps or occasionally in tents. On "primitive trail" trips you're required to carry your own bags and sleep under the stars (primitive trails don't use tents). This is an extreme option and is not the most common type of walking safari.

Making Tracks

Popular places for walking safaris include the Umfolozi Wilderness Area of South Africa's Hluhluwe-Umfolozi Game Reserve, where wilderness trails were pioneered; Tanzania's Selous Game Reserve, on treks run by Sand River Lodge; and Zambia's South Luangwa National Park, on Robin Pope Safaris treks. The wilderness trails in public Kruger National Park, where national-park rangers guide you, are also quite good; trails need to be reserved 13 months in advance when bookings first become available. In Zimbabwe the most notable walking options are in Mana Pools National Park, on the Lower Zambezi River. Zimbabwe is the only country in Africa with an association for professional guides and hunters; the association's guides have to pass the most rigorous tracking and bush-craft tests in Africa.

If you consider a walking safari, you must factor in your physical condition. You should be in good health and be able to walk between 4 and 10 mi a day, depending on the parameters of the trip. Some trips don't allow hikers under age 12 or over age 60. Also, you shouldn't scare easily. No guide has time for people who freeze up at the sight of a beetle, spider, or something more menacing up close; guides need to keep their attention on the wilds around them and on the group as a whole. The

TREADING LIGHTLY

What is true ecotourism? It's difficult to say because the term is widely used but lacks a widely accepted definition. In general, however, ecotourism aims to expose travelers to natural areas, preferably those areas practicing sustainable land use while conserving these very places; to educate travelers about the physical and/or cultural environment of these areas; and to bring about positive developments for the local communities. Not every safari strives to achieve all these goals.

Definitions aside, you should, on a basic level, care and be informed about the environment and the people you visit, particularly in places where living conditions are poor. What can you do? For starters, ask your tour operator and safari outfitter for specifics about how their trips are run and what their relationship is to the local communities where the trips are held. You can also ask specific questions about ecological measures, such as whether the lodges utilize solar power and conserve water. Don't litter, pay too much or little for services and curios or souvenirs (ask locals for advice), or feed wild animals. If you'd like to help local conservation efforts or support local communities, ask about funds and trusts set up by safari operators and make a donation. And try to heed the ethic of taking only photographs and leaving only your footprints— but do have fun along the way.

guides are armed and they take great caution to keep you away from trouble. Sometimes, however, trouble comes looking for you, so you are expected to shoulder a good deal of the burden in terms of your behavior. Your best insurance against getting in harm's way is to always listen to your guide and follow instructions.

HORSE SAFARIS

There's no better way to see game than on horseback. Because many wild animals regard a rider and mount as one of them, on horse you can come quite close to most plains game—antelope, zebras, giraffes—and, on occasion, join a herd as you ride. In certain circumstances you may even be able to approach, cautiously and quietly, elephants and buffalo herds. You also can cover a lot of ground quickly and get out of tight spots in a flash.

Horseback riders are well aware of the pure pleasure of riding and the archetypal communion between human and horse; in the bush, with its attendant dangers and mysteries, the experience is greatly heightened. In addition, group camaraderie tends to be much more intense on a riding safari than on other kinds of safaris. You soon learn, for instance, the unwritten law that whoever loses her hat while riding buys drinks that night.

Because of the nature of the terrain and the unpredictable behavior of wild animals, these trips are appropriate only for proficient riders. On some horse safaris you ride out from a permanent tented bush camp, which serves as your base. On wilderness horse trails you move to a different bush camp each night; this option is usually recommended only for experienced riders, who can handle themselves in tricky situations.

Most horse safaris are fully catered and accompanied by a groom who tends the horses with great care. You're expected to take an interest in your horse and, on wilderness trails, to help pack up temporary camps; saddling up yourself is always appreciated, but your guide will first want to see that you can do it properly. Then there's the night watch. Lions love horse meat, so when in lion country the members of your group will take turns on watch through the night. You'll relive these unique nights in the bush for many years to come.

Book your trip with an operator who belongs to the Association of Southern and East African Horse-Safari Operators, a by-invitation-only group (not every horse-safari operator is a member). In most cases you need to bring your own riding clothes, including chaps.

CANOE SAFARIS

Intrepid canoe operators pioneered canoe safaris in the late 1970s and early 1980s on the wild Zambezi River. Today these safaris are one of the most popular ways to see the wildlife around the Zambezi, which forms the border between Zambia and Zimbabwe. The Zambezi River passes through some of the finest big-game areas in Africa, including Mana Pools National

Park in Zimbabwe and Lower Zambezi National Park in Zambia, as well as the parks' bordering "game management" (a.k.a. hunting) areas. You can see hippos and crocodiles as well as elephants, buffalo, lions and other predators, and plenty of birds, all at a unique ground-level angle. The South Luangwa River, a tributary of the Zambezi in Zambia, is an option solely for experienced canoers.

A canoe safari may sound sedate—floating down the river in a two-person canoe, stopping on the banks to take refreshments and to camp—but the rowing can be strenuous, and you do have to be on the alert for wild animals. The rowing is tougher from August to October, when strong headwinds can blow, sometimes for days, and make the water choppy. To go on a canoe safari, you should be fairly fit and healthy and know how to swim.

A Day on the River

The more expensive canoe safaris are fully catered, whereas the less-expensive options are participatory, which means you chip in with camp chores. Most activities are on the water, and the idea is to get going early and hit the water right after breakfast. You always have time for a short walk around camp, however, and some bird-watching.

Then you paddle. And you paddle. Because the banks of the Zambezi and other big rivers are busy with game activity, there's always something to see. Rivers in safari areas teem with hippos and crocodiles, which together account for more deaths in Africa than any other large animals, so you must be alert even on the laziest, hottest afternoon.

Breaks are taken before and after lunch and sometimes include a short walk through riverine forest with your armed guide. Lunch is a more leisurely stop, during which you rest, enjoy landfall, and socialize. You reach your overnight site in mid- to late afternoon, set up camp, and then take a game walk for an hour or two until it's time to head back to freshen up for dinner. Hot "bucket" showers are normally provided. After dinner it's time for fireside tales before you head to bed to rest up so you can do it all over again in the morning.

MOBILE & OVERLAND SAFARIS

In places such as Botswana and Namibia, where in the 1970s and '80s hunting concessions controlled the best safari areas, so-called photographic-safari operators gained access to these areas by special four-wheel-drive vehicles. And thus the mobile, or literally overland, safari was born. Travel was usually in specially adapted Land Rovers and, later, Toyota Land Cruisers that were fitted with extra seats, long-range fuel tanks, high canopies, and large windows. You'd climb aboard in Johannesburg, Windhoek, or Harare and head off into the bush with your guide, who invariably had long hair, a beard, and a twinkle in his eye.

Many Southern Africans first experienced a safari in a four-wheel-drive vehicle. Favorite destinations were the Central Kalahari and "the Swamps," as the Okavango Delta was then known, and the other places on the way, including the Makgadikgadi Pans, Nxai Pan, Lake Ngami, Savuti, Chobe, Victoria Falls . . . many still favorite destinations in Southern Africa.

Today most mobile-safari operations are expertly run but are nevertheless budget options. Some of those twinkle-eyed young guides eventually bought out or outbid the hunting concessions and now have thriving safari businesses—Game Trackers, Karibu, Penduka, and Wilderness Safaris, to name a few.

Mobile excursions are mostly self-sufficient camping affairs with overnights at either public or private campgrounds, depending on the safari's itinerary and price. Sometimes, as is the case with Drifters Adventours, which owns several low-end lodges throughout Southern Africa, you stay at basic lodges along the way. Travel is often by something that looks like a four-wheel-drive bus.

For young people, or the young at heart, mobile safaris are a great way to see the land from ground level. You taste the dust, smell the bacon cooking, stop where and when you want (within reason), and get to see the best places in the region. Many of these trips are aimed at budget-conscious travelers; prices are especially low if you choose to travel by the seat of your pants and book with a local operator after arriving in South Africa.

Trips usually run 14 to 21 days, although you can find shorter ones that cover fewer destinations. Prices start at US$750 and climb to US$2,500 all-inclusive. Not sure whether this is right for you? Consider combining a mobile safari with a lodge-based one, which gives you the best of both worlds. A minimum of 10 nights is recommended for such an itinerary.

The Mobile Way of Life

You sleep in "fly camps"—groups of small tents you pitch yourself—that are set up in a new location at the end of every day. In the morning you have time for a steaming cup of coffee or tea before departing at dawn on a game drive. You have to pack before you leave for the morning drive because while you're out, breakfast is being prepared and the camp broken down.

A grand breakfast (you'll be amazed what can come out of a simple camp kitchen) awaits your return from the game drive, which usually takes a few hours. Then you're off, driving leisurely through the African wilds and toward your next overnight destination, which you reach by early afternoon. Lunch is normally a snack at a scenic spot en route. Sometimes you can take a guided game walk in the afternoon; otherwise, you have an hour or two to rest before the evening game drive.

When you return, there's time to freshen up with a hot bucket shower (a pecking order quickly asserts itself as to who goes first and last), and then it's time for dinner under the stars. A proper table is laid, right down to wineglasses and chilled beer.

These nights around the campfire, with the sounds of the night creatures, the smell of acacia-wood smoke, and the dazzling ceiling of the Milky Way, will remain with you for a long, long time.

SELF-DRIVE SAFARIS

A self-drive safari, where you drive yourself in your own rental car, is a great option for budget travelers and for those who feel comfortable seeing the bush without a ranger at hand to search out game or explain what you're seeing. The two most popular and easiest-to-navigate options for this kind of trip are Kruger National Park in South Africa and Etosha National Park in Namibia. These two parks have paved, well-marked roads and a wide range of accommodations that include family-size chalets, small huts, tents, and hostel-like dorms. You may buy your own groceries and cook for yourself at all of these areas; some options, especially in Kruger, have restaurants and small stores on-site.

A two-wheel-drive car is fine, and you can stop and start at your leisure; remember that you have to stick to marked roads. As well as patience, you'll need drinks, snacks, and loads of film. Keep your eyes and ears open and you may come across game at any time, in any place.

CAMEL & ELEPHANT SAFARIS

In dry, northern Kenya and Namibia's Namib Desert, you can travel through the bush on a camel, fantasizing that you're an Arabian nomad on an African adventure. Namibian camel safaris are essentially riding ones and last one to two weeks. In Samburu National Reserve in Kenya, you're mostly on foot while the camels carry supplies or tired walkers.

At Abu Camp in Botswana's Okavango, Wild Horizons' Elephant Camp near Victoria Falls, and Kapama Lodge in the South African Lowveld, you can see the bush from the back of an elephant. Although you start off from the base lodge riding, all elephant safaris require some walking. The younger the elephant, the more you have to walk, and sometimes you might be on foot half the time. The highlight of riding an elephant is that you can really get in among the other game. It's also thrilling to walk with these huge and truly awesome creatures. When booking one of these safaris, read the fine print carefully. Many lodges offer one-day elephant-encounter experiences, which, although soul stirring in their own right, don't constitute what is generally understood to be a safari—a journey or at least a multiday experience.

There are no specific fitness or weight restrictions for camel and elephant safaris. That said, you should be in reasonably good shape. Getting on and off an elephant requires basic physical adroitness; camel rides are bumpy and often uncomfortable, and they require you to employ muscles you probably don't use normally. In addition, walking in the bush can be hot and tiring.

Camel & Elephant Excursions

Mornings are spent in camp, either a permanent lodge or tents. After breakfast you head out for a game drive, but with camels and elephants instead of safari vehicles. On an elephant safari you either spend the day away from camp, taking lunch alfresco in the bush, or you return to the camp for the midday meal. On a camel trip you spend one or more days away from camp, much like you would on a horseback safari.

The beauty of this type of safari is that you can combine riding and walking. The walking may not sound as exciting as the riding, but after the novelty of riding these beasts wears off—about the time your backside goes numb and your legs go into spasms—you'll probably want to get down to ground level anyway.

4

Before You Leave

You've picked your safari location and firmed up your travel plans. Now it's time to start your detail planning. You need to organize your papers, create thorough packing lists, and do more homework on your destination. You also should research the currency used and international exchange rates, tipping practices, health precautions, photographic needs, and the weather. If you take the time to manage the details before you leave, the only bumps on your safari should be in your 4×4 as you traverse the African bush.

THE PAPER TRAIL

You need a valid passport to travel to any African country. If you don't have a passport, apply immediately because the process takes approximately five to six weeks. For a greatly increased fee, the application process can be shortened to as little as one week, but leaving this detail to the last minute can be stressful. If you have a passport, check the expiration date; if it's due to expire within six months of your return date, you need to renew your passport at once. Certain countries, such as South Africa, won't let you enter with a soon-to-expire passport; you also need two blank pages in your passport to enter South Africa.

If you're headed to Kenya, Tanzania, Zambia, or Zimbabwe, you need a visa. In most cases you obtain the application by contacting the embassy or consulate. About two months before your departure, you must submit to the embassy or consulate the completed application, your passport, two passport-size photos of yourself, and a copy of your round-trip air ticket. The photos should be notarized and signed by you on the back. In some cases you may also be required to show proof of sufficient funds to pay for your vacation and your way home. You can arrange with your travel agent or outfitter to provide a supporting letter saying that you have sufficient funds and to provide a copy of the round-trip or onward air ticket. It's better to be prepared than to be denied entry into a country—and lose not only your vacation, but your money as well—for a bit of paperwork.

DOCUMENT CHECKLIST

- [ ] Passport
- [ ] Visas, if necessary
- [ ] Airline tickets
- [ ] Proof of yellow-fever inoculation
- [ ] Accommodation and transfer vouchers
- [ ] Car-rental reservation forms
- [ ] International driver's license
- [ ] Copy of information page of your passport
- [ ] Copy of airline tickets
- [ ] Copy of medical prescriptions
- [ ] Copy of traveler's check numbers
- [ ] List of credit-card numbers and international contact information for each card issuer
- [ ] Copy of travel insurance and medical-emergency evacuation policy
- [ ] Travel agent's contact numbers
- [ ] A letter of consent from one parent if the other parent is traveling alone with their children

When mailing your passport to an embassy or consulate with a visa request, send it via registered mail or courier service; request a signature upon delivery to ensure tracking in the event of a lost passport. Keep copies of all documents you submit, including your passport, and make copies of visas once you have them.

When you collect your passport with visa inside (stuck or stamped), you normally have to pay a small fee. A valuable service offered by your travel agent or tour operator is the ability to secure all the visas you need for your safari without your having to personally visit an embassy or consulates or fill out reams of paperwork. Your travel agent may refer you to a visa service that handles the entire process for a fee. Either way, let the professionals do the work for you; you may end up saving yourself an aspirin-bottle's worth of headaches.

Check on what immunizations are required for the countries you're visiting. Although proof of inoculation against yellow fever was required in the past for many destinations, American citizens traveling in Africa currently need vaccination proof only in Tanzania. However, other countries (especially Kenya and Uganda) may demand an inoculation certificate if you arrive directly from a tropical area or have traveled to one prior to your safari trip.

If you're taking a self-driving safari in a national park or will be renting a car before or after your safari in countries other than South Africa and Namibia, you need an international driver's license. These licenses are valid for one year and are issued while you wait at any American Automobile Association (AAA) office in the United States; you must have a current U.S. driver's license. You need to bring two passport-type photographs with you for the license. A valid U.S. driver's license is accepted in South Africa and Namibia.

PREPARING TO GO

	PASSPORT	VISA
South Africa	√	no
Namibia	√	no
Botswana	√	no
Zimbabwe	√	√ - US$30
Zambia	√	√ - US$30 plus US$10 for each dependent; US$40 at entry point
Malawi	√	no
Tanzania	√	√ - US$50
Kenya	√	√ - US$50
Uganda	√	√ - US$30

*Only Tanzania requires U.S. citizens to have a valid yellow-fever inoculation certificate. However, any one of these other countries may require such a certificate if you are arriving from, or have traveled to, any third-world or tropical or sub-tropical area prior to your safari trip.

**Onward or return trip.

TIP If you're planning a honeymoon safari, make sure the bride's airline ticket, passport, and visas all use the same last name. Any discrepancies, especially between a passport and an airline ticket, will result in your trip being grounded before you ever take off. Brides may want to consider waiting to change their last name until after the honeymoon.

HEALTH PRECAUTIONS*	ON/RET** TICKET	SUPPORT FUNDS
malaria (Lowveld parks only)	√	√
malaria	√	√
malaria	√	√
malaria	√	√
malaria	no	no
malaria	no	no
malaria, yellow fever	no	no
malaria, yellow fever	√	no
malaria, yellow fever	no	no

TRAVEL INSURANCE

Get a comprehensive travel-insurance policy in addition to any primary insurance you already have. Travel insurance incorporates trip cancellation; trip interruption or travel delay; loss or theft of, or damage to, baggage; baggage delay; medical expenses; emergency medical transportation; and collision damage waiver if renting a car. These policies are offered by most travel-insurance companies in one comprehensive policy and vary in price based on both your total trip cost and your age.

Many travel agents and tour operators stipulate that travel insurance is mandatory if you book your trip through them. This coverage is not only for your financial protection in the event of a cancellation but also for coverage of medical emergencies and medical evacuations due to injury or illness, which often involve use of jet aircraft with hospital equipment and doctors on board and can amount to many thousands of dollars.

If you need emergency medical evacuation, most travel-insurance companies stipulate that you *must* obtain authorization by the company *prior to* the evacuation. Unfortunately, many safari camps and lodges are so remote that they don't have access to a telephone, so getting prior authorization is extremely difficult if not impossible. You should check with your insurance company before you leave to see whether it has this clause and if so, what can be done to get around it. Good travel agents and tour operators are aware of the issue and will address it.

TIP Purchase travel insurance within seven days of paying your initial trip deposit. For most policies this will not only insure your trip deposit, but also cover you for any preexisting medical conditions and default by most airlines and safari companies. The latter two are not covered if your policy is purchased after seven days.

PACKING SMART

For the most part African safari destinations are tropical and warm in the daytime. Temperatures range from 75°F to 95°F. However, parts of Southern Africa—particularly Botswana, eastern Zimbabwe, and the Namibian desert—can be extremely cold on winter evenings and mornings, plunging to 10°F (-12°C). The best game-viewing season is mid- to late winter, so you should pack some warm clothes with your safari khakis.

Light, neutral-color clothes are universally worn on safari. Khaki-color clothing was first used in Africa as camouflage by the South African Boers, and then by the British army that fought them during the Boer War. The khaki color replaced the famously conspicuous red coats of the British and helped them blend into the open veld. Light colors also help to deflect the harsh sun and, unlike dark colors, are less likely to attract mosquitoes.

Start with these basics when you're packing: for summer, two pairs of shorts (skirts or sarongs—called *kikois* in Kenya—are great, too); two T-shirts or short-sleeve khaki shirts; two long-sleeve lightweight shirts for sun and bug protection; two pairs of long pants; sandals;

sneakers or light boots, depending on what type of safari you're taking; a sun hat or baseball cap; and a light rain jacket or Windbreaker. Women may want to consider packing a support or sports bra. On some safaris, dinners are dressy; ask your travel agent about what to expect, and pack appropriately. In winter, eliminate the shorts and add a warm jacket, a sweater or sweatshirt (lightweight and warm, fleece is an especially good choice), gloves, and a warm hat. Because of recent guerrilla bush wars in Africa, and due to its association with hunting, jungle camouflage clothing isn't appropriate for a photographic safari. In some countries, including South Africa, it is banned for reasons of security.

Think twice about packing blue jeans. For one, denim is heavy and therefore takes a long time to dry if you're having laundry done in the bush. Also, in areas where tsetse flies occur, the traps used to lure the insects are a dark blue color, similar to the dye of many jeans. It's possible that in these locations your jeans could make you a tsetse-fly target.

You should need only three changes of clothing for an entire trip; almost all safaris include laundry as part of the package. If you're self-driving you can carry more, but washing is still easy and three changes of clothes should be ample if you use drip-dry fabrics that need no ironing. Note that in certain countries—Botswana, for example—the staff won't wash underwear because it's against their custom. On mobile safaris you're expected to wear tops and bottoms more than once, and either bring enough underwear to last a week between lodges, or wash as you go in the bathroom sink. In summer, clothes dry overnight in the hot African air.

On a canoe safari you're in the relentless sun every day and have to protect your legs, especially the tops of your thighs and shins, from sunburn. Bring a towel or, even better, a kikoi or sarong and place it over your legs. Sunscreen of SPF 30 or higher is de rigueur.

Many safari operators offer the option of going on a game walk in addition to, or instead of, a game drive. Pack sturdy but light walking shoes or boots—in most cases durable sneakers suffice for this option. For a walking-based safari, you need sturdy, lightweight boots. Buy them well in advance of your trip so you have time to break them in.

If you're going to walk in the bush remember that it's full of tiny things that crawl and bite. Spray insect repellent on your shoes, socks, and legs up to your knees, even if you're wearing pants, before you set off for a game walk or evening drive. If you've been out on a walk it's a good idea to take a hot shower and soap your entire body when you return. Also, if possible, isolate the clothes used on your walk from the remainder of the clean garments in your bag. Bring a couple of large white plastic garbage bags for dirty laundry.

Most hotels and game lodges provide toiletries such as soap, shampoo, and insect repellent, so you don't need to overpack these items. In the larger lodges in South Africa, in the national parks as well the private game reserves, stores and gift shops are fairly well stocked with clothing, film, and guidebooks; in self-drive and -catering areas, shops also carry food and drink. In Botswana, lodges that belong to groups such as Wilderness Safaris or Game Trackers have small shops with a limited selection of books, clothing, film, and trinkets. In East Africa all large hotel-style lodges such as those in the Serena and Sopa groups have fairly well-stocked shops. Elsewhere in Africa you're not likely to find this type of amenity on safari.

As for any trip, remember that the lighter you pack the easier it will be to carry your luggage. If you're flying to safari destinations with regular airports where large airplanes are used—Arusha Airport or Kilimanjaro International Airport in Tanzania; Wilson Airport, outside Nairobi; or Hoedspruit or Kruger Park Airport, both in South Africa—normal international airline baggage allowances apply. Otherwise, access to game-viewing areas is often by light aircraft, on short sandy landing strips; therefore, luggage weight restrictions are strictly enforced. You'll be allowed one duffel-type bag, approximately 36 inches by 18 inches, so that it can be easily packed into the baggage pods of a small plane. One small camera and personal-effects bag can go on your lap. Keep all your documents and money in this personal bag.

Do yourself a favor and leave breakables and valuables at home. If you'd be heartbroken if an item was broken or lost, it probably doesn't belong on a safari.

TIP Tinted fashion glasses are in most cases not strong enough for the harsh African sunlight. When

PACKING CHECKLIST

- ☐ Two cotton T-shirts
- ☐ Two long-sleeve cotton shirts
- ☐ Two pairs shorts or two skirts in summer
- ☐ Two pairs long pants (three pairs in winter)
- ☐ Optional: Sweatshirt and pants, which can double as sleepwear
- ☐ Optional: A dressy dinner outfit
- ☐ Underwear and socks
- ☐ Walking shoes or sneakers
- ☐ Sandals
- ☐ Bathing suit
- ☐ Warm sweater in winter
- ☐ Windbreaker or rain poncho
- ☐ Camera equipment, plenty of film, and extra batteries
- ☐ Contact lenses, including extras
- ☐ Eyeglasses
- ☐ Binoculars
- ☐ Personal toiletries
- ☐ Malaria tablets
- ☐ Sunscreen and lip balm with SPF 30 or higher, moisturizer, and hair conditioner
- ☐ Antihistamine cream
- ☐ Insect repellent with minimum 30% DEET
- ☐ Basic first-aid kit (aspirin, bandages, anti-diarrheal, antiseptic cream, etc.)

- ☐ Tissues and/or premoistened wipes
- ☐ Hat, scarf, and gloves (for winter)
- ☐ Sun hat and sunglasses
- ☐ Documents and money (cash, traveler's checks, credit cards), etc.
- ☐ A notebook and pens
- ☐ Travel and field guides
- ☐ A couple of large white plastic garbage bags
- ☐ U.S. dollars in small denominations ($1, $5, $10) for tipping

shopping for sunglasses purchase Polaroid and UV-protected ones.

Plug It In

Most of Southern Africa is on 220/240 volt alternating current (AC). The plug points are round. However, there are both large 15-amp three-prong sockets (with a ground connection) and smaller two-prong 5-amp sockets. In East Africa the current is also 220/240 volt AC, but plug points are British-type three-pin square. Most lodges have adapter plugs, especially for recharging of video batteries; check before you go, or purchase a universal plug adapter before you leave home.

Safari hotels in the Serengeti or Masai Mara, the private reserve areas outside Kruger National Park, and the less-rustic private lodges in South Africa are likely to provide you with plug points and plugs, and some offer hair dryers and electric-razor sockets as well (check this before you go). Lodges on limited generator and solar power are usually able to charge video batteries, so long as you have the right plug.

Binoculars

Many creatures and plants living in the bush are smaller than an elephant or a lion. You'll miss thousands of birds, small meerkats, tortoises, dung beetles, and tree species without a pair of binoculars. Binoculars help you get a close look at an elephant's hide or tick birds at work on a giraffe's neck; plus, from a greater distance you'll be able to watch larger animals behaving in a totally unhindered way.

Although your guide may have binoculars in the safari vehicle, don't count on being able to borrow them at the precise moment an African eagle takes off from its nest or when a leopard is spotted in a tree 300 yards away. One of Africa's greatest attractions is its birdlife, and seasoned safari goers can be identified by the binoculars slung around their necks and the bird field guides in their hands. You'll gain an entirely new perspective on the bush with binoculars at hand. Many people find that when they start using binoculars and stop documenting each trip detail on film, they have a much better safari experience.

Binoculars come in many types and sizes, and you basically get what you pay for. Avoid buying a cheap pair because the optics will be poor and the lenses usually don't stay aligned for long (especially if they get bumped, which they will on safari). The most expensive binoculars have specially tinted lenses and are auto focusing; these are a great option if they fit into your budget. For game viewing, compact binoculars are fine, but for birds you might want a larger pair.

The minimum size you should consider is around 7×30 (this means the magnification is seven times and the diameter of the lens, which determines how bright the image will be, is 30 mm). Up to 10×60 is good, but larger sizes can become too heavy to use for any length of time. If binoculars are not light enough to hold steady for a good while, they will start shaking and will magnify not only the image but also the shake, making them difficult to use in a moving vehicle.

HEALTH FACTORS

Africa is home to just about every human-borne disease and ailment; however, this doesn't mean you're at risk when you travel on the continent, especially if you stick to the cities and safari lodges. The real danger is malaria. But by taking the necessary precautions you should be well protected.

Malaria

Malaria is the most common parasitic infection in the world. It infects 300 million to 500 million people each year in some 90 countries of the tropical and subtropical regions of the globe and kills between 1.5 million and 3 million. Malaria infects about 10,000 returning travelers each year and is fatal to about 1% of them. However, malaria is preventable and shouldn't prevent you from going on safari.

Malaria occurs throughout the tropics and in adjacent hot and low-lying areas. The disease is spread by the female Anopheles mosquito, which is infected with the malaria parasite. She spreads it by picking it up from an already infected person and passing it on when she next feeds on the high-protein blood she needs to reproduce.

This female Anopheles mosquito is the ultimate insect Stealth fighter plane; she is shy and feeds only between dusk and dawn, usually after midnight when you are most soundly asleep. She is almost silent when she flies and she homes in mainly on your exhaled carbon dioxide and body warmth. When she locates you, this pesky little critter can spend hours searching for access to your skin, such as a small hole or gap in the overlap of your mosquito net. If you have been infected, you can expect to feel the effects anywhere from 7 to 90 days afterward. Typically you will feel like you have the flu, with worsening high fever, chills and sweats, headache, and muscle aches. In some cases this is accompanied by abdominal pain, diarrhea, and a cough. If it's not treated you could die.

PROTECTING YOURSELF The best way to protect yourself against malaria is to avoid getting bitten in the first place. Start your precautions by treating your clothes with a mosquito-repellent spray or laundry wash before you leave home. Most of these last approximately 14 days and through several washings and contain the active ingredient permethrin, which is sold as Permanone and Duranon. This spray is specifically for clothes and shouldn't be used on skin. You can find it at camping and outdoor stores such as Eastern Mountain Sports. Mosquitoes (and tsetse flies) are attracted to dark surfaces, where they're hard to detect, so wear light-color clothing while on safari. Make sure your skin is covered with clothing in the morning and evening, and tuck your pants into your socks so your ankles aren't exposed. Use a mosquito-repellent spray that contains DEET on all exposed skin, unless you're pregnant or nursing. DEET also is not recommended for children. Citronella and other natural bug repellents can be used, but they're not as potent and require more-vigilant use. Most safari lodges have fans over, or facing, the bed. This is one of the best ways to thwart mosquitoes because they can't fly well in moving air. If you're not in an air-conditioned room or insect-proofed place, try to wash your mosquito net in permethrin, too.

There's no vaccine against malaria, but there are several medications you can use to protect yourself from getting the disease. In the United States, mefloquine (known as Lariam) was the most widely used antimalarial until relatively recently. Although the active ingredient mefloquine works well against the disease, it can have strong side effects, such as depression, nightmares, and hallucinations. And it shouldn't be used by anyone on any other medication, including birth-control hormones. Chloroquine and Malarone are currently the most recommended anti-malaria medications in the United States. They are easy to take and have few known side effects.

Consult a doctor who has knowledge of malarial areas to prescribe the correct medication. If you live in an area without a tropical-disease specialist, consult the Centers for Disease Control and Prevention (CDC) Web site for more information. It's vital that you take the prescribed dosage and the full course of the anti-malarial medication because the incubation period for malaria can last up to four weeks after your return. Not taking even the last tablet of a multiweek course can mask the disease for several months; when it does erupt it will be more advanced and harder to detect than if you had followed the full regimen.

It's possible to treat malaria after you have contracted it, but this shouldn't be your long-term strategy for dealing with the disease.

PROTECTING YOUR CHILDREN The first malarial protection method is to practice "safe safari"—that is, avoid getting bitten. This can be done by treating children's clothes in an insect-repellent soap; covering exposed skin with insect repellent every morning and evening; dressing children in long pants, long-sleeve shirts, and shoes and socks in the mornings and evenings; using mosquito coils and sprays in your rooms; and sleeping under mosquito nets. Many Southern Africans prefer to do all of the above rather than take strong anti-malaria drugs, and if you are

100% vigilant, this tack can work. The CDC recommends that children traveling to a malarial area see a doctor four to six weeks prior to the trip. There are several prescription anti-malaria drugs, including mefloquine and Malarone, that have been approved by the CDC for use by children.

Both the effects of malaria and the side effects of malarial prophylactics put strain on young kidneys. For this and other health reasons, it's best not to visit malarial areas with children under age 10 unless you practice stringent nonchemical preventive measures. Malaria's effects on young children are much worse than they are on older people.

Another, easier option is to choose a nonmalarial safari destination. Malaria-free destinations include Skeleton Coast and Etosha Pan in Namibia and high-altitude sections of Kenya and Tanzania.

TIP If you feel ill even several months after you return home, tell your doctor that you have been in a malaria-infected area. The onset of flulike symptoms—aching joints or headache—is often the first sign that you have contracted either tick-bite fever (a bacterial infection transmitted by ticks with symptoms including fever, severe headache, and a rash consisting of small red bumps) or malaria. Take it very seriously and go for a blood test immediately.

Other African Health Issues

Yellow fever isn't inherent in any of the countries discussed in this book; only Tanzania requires all visitors to be inoculated against the disease and to show proof of inoculation. Southern and East African countries may, however, require you to present a valid yellow-fever inoculation certificate if prior to arrival you traveled to a region infected with yellow fever. The CDC recommends that you get vaccinated for yellow fever before traveling to Tanzania, Kenya, and other sub-Saharan countries to protect your health, and also advises to get a certificate of vaccination and keep it with you in case you're asked to produce it. An inoculation provides immunity for 10 years.

Hepatitis A can be transmitted via contaminated seafood, water, or fruits and vegetables. According to the CDC, hepatitis A is the most common vaccine-preventable disease in travelers. Immunization consists of a series of two shots received six months apart. You need to have received only the first one before you travel. This should be given at least four weeks before your trip.

The CDC recommends vaccination for hepatitis B only if you might be exposed to blood (for example, health-care workers), have sexual contact with the local population, stay longer than six months, or be exposed through medical treatment. As needed, you should receive booster shots for tetanus-diphtheria (every 10 years), measles (you're usually immunized as a child), and polio (you're usually immunized as a child).

All reputable hotels and lodges have either filtered, clean tap water, or provide sterilized drinking water in jugs. However, the natural microfauna and -flora differ in every region, and if you drink local, nonfiltered water, add ice to your soda in the airport, or eat a piece of fruit from a roadside stand, you may get what's commonly referred to as traveler's diarrhea. If you're unsure of local water supplies, carry bottled water. Nearly all camps and lodges have adequate supplies of bottled water, and in some cases it's included in the cost of your trip. If you're going on a mobile safari, ask your guide whether drinking water is available; if you're self-driving, stock up on bottled water and other drinks in towns. If you're traveling outside of organized safari camps in rural Africa, follow the CDC's advice for fruits and vegetables: boil it, cook it, peel it, or forget it.

CAMERA SMARTS

All the safaris included in this book are photographic safaris; the goal is to preserve the images of your trip on film. That said, if you spend your entire safari with one eye closed and the other peering through a camera lens, you may miss all the other sensual elements that contribute to the great show that is the African bush. And more than likely, your pictures won't look like the photos you see in books about African safaris. A professional photographer can spend a full year in the field to produce a book, so you are often better off just taking snaps of your trip and buying a book to take home.

There's no shortage of first-class coffee-table books on the African bush. Once, when asked how he was able to capture the images he did, a wildlife photographer answered "five miles." He had calculated that he'd shot five miles of 35mm film in his professional life (at a cost of around US$200,000 for the film and processing).

Whatever type of photographer you are, the secret to taking great pictures has three components: first is always good light. An hour after sunrise and before sunset are the magic times for good light; for the few hours of harsh light each side of midday, you might as well put your camera away. The second component is framing: a head or a tail goes out of frame, or with auto-focus cameras the head is always framed dead center and no care is taken about the rest of the composition. The third component is capturing sharp images: use a tripod or the safari equivalent, a beanbag, to rest the camera on while in a vehicle. When using a long lens (upward of 200mm), you cannot hand-hold a steady shot; you must have some support if you want your photos to be clear.

Take lots of film with you because it's not always available on safaris. Also, take spare batteries; two sets of spares if you're going for longer than a week.

Because of the dust, especially in Namibia, you should keep all electronic equipment in sealed plastic bags while you're traveling, and have one or more cloth covers while you're working. Clean your equipment every day if you can.

POINTERS FOR AMATEUR PHOTOGRAPHERS If you have anything less than the equivalent of a

200–300mm f2.8 lens on a high-quality camera body (preferably auto-focus), concentrate on taking photographs of the people, camps, and landscapes (with animals in them), rather than wasting your time trying to take good wildlife shots. For all close-up work with people, even in broad daylight, you should use a camera flash (strobe) for fill-in light. Modern camera flashes have an automatic TTL (through the lens) mode, which is the one you should use. You'll be amazed at the excellent results. For point-and-shoot cameras, use 100 or 200 ASA print film; Fuji, Kodak, and Agfa are recommended brands. To capture Africa's vistas, pack a couple of disposable cameras that allow you to take panoramic shots.

POINTERS FOR PHOTOGRAPHY ENTHUSIASTS

An African safari gives you the opportunity to have a lot of fun with landscape pictures, animal action shots, and close-up or macro snaps of insects and plants. Compiling all the camera components is expensive. The ideal camera kit consists of an auto-focus body (such as a Nikon F80, F90, or F100—or an F5 for the real pros, or the Canon Eos range) and three or four lenses. Start with a wide-angle 20mm lens, a "standard" lens of 28–80 or 35–105, a long lens from 400mm to 600mm, and a close-up lens such as a 105mm macro. Then you want a dedicated (automatic) flash, a back-up camera body (if you can), and lots of cleaning equipment.

You can cut your kit down to fewer lenses by playing with the combination of zoom lenses, depending on your budget and what is available. Most important, buy the best lenses you can rather than the best camera body. The faster the lens the more expensive and the better it is (the f-stop rating tells you how fast it can shoot). F2.8 is ideal for wildlife; anything slower than f5.6 starts getting too slow for moving subjects and low-light conditions.

Film choice is a personal preference, but most professionals prefer Fuji Velvia slide (transparency or color reversal) film rated at 50 ASA. Fuji Provia or Sensia slide film at 100 ASA is better for general use. Kodak 100 ASA and Ektachrome 50 ASA are the other options for serious photographers, but unless you want to project or publish your work, you should consider print film. Here Fuji and Kodak have equally good products. Remember, though, the slower your lens the faster you'll want your film speed to be; but the faster the film speed, the grainier the picture—which is why the pros use slow film and fast lenses.

TIP Consider taking two basic filters to make the most of difficult lighting conditions: this is not to make use of gimmicks like false colors, but to deepen the natural colors and reduce the glare of overexposure of certain areas. The first is a circular polarizer for auto-focus cameras or a linear polarizer for manual-focus cameras, which allow you to take acceptable photos even in the harshest light. You can increase or decrease the amount of polarizing by turning the outer ring. A graduated gray filter placed in front of your lens darkens bright skies and thus evens the exposure between land and sky—a common failing of photographs. Then bring a soft warming filter, just to give a slightly warmer mood when the natural light isn't flattering.

Digital Cameras

A good alternative to conventional photography equipment is a digital camera, especially if you have a personal computer with image-enhancing software such as Photoshop. Good digital cameras are still much more expensive than 35mm SLR cameras (single-lens reflex—the standard kind), and the memory cards or sticks are pricey. But the benefits of being able to preview shots, selecting what you want and deleting what you don't, storing them, and then adjusting them on a computer can outweigh the initial cost.

The resolution of nonprofessional digital cameras is approaching that of good film. Cameras with eight megapixels of resolution can print high-quality, smooth A4 or letter-size prints. Images with five-megapixel resolution are fine as well. Invest in a telephoto lens to shoot wildlife—this may mean upgrading to a more robust camera. Buy or borrow as many memory cards as you can. You may want to use multiple smaller memory cards to minimalize the risk of losing dozens of images. And, as always, bring extra batteries.

Video Cameras

Video cameras these days are almost universally digital. The benefits of video are threefold: it's much easier to get basically pleasing results with moving images than with still photography; video cameras are much more light-sensitive than still cameras, so you can shoot in much lower light conditions; and you can edit your tapes and show them on your VCR at home. There's also the added benefit of the amazing zoom-lens capability on most video cameras, which can give you almost as close a look at large animals as with binoculars (the zoom doesn't work as well with smaller, far-off subjects). And what's more, a good compact digital video camera costs much less than a good 35mm SLR or a still digital camera. Video cameras are hungry for batteries, however, and you may run into recharging problems in remote safari destinations.

Another problem with video cameras (but not for the person behind the lens) is that persistent videographers can become annoying to the other people in a group, so be sensitive about this; don't go everywhere with your camera glued to your eye while simultaneously issuing nonstop commentary. Eventually someone is going to tell you to plug it, or worse. Resist poking your lens close to strangers' faces—it looks great through the lens but these are not paid actors, and they'll appreciate being given their own space.

MONEY MATTERS

Most safaris are paid for in advance, so you need money only to cover personal purchases and gratuities. (The cash you take should include small denominations, i.e., US$1, US$5, and US$10, for tips.) If you're not on a packaged tour and are self-driving, you need to carry more money. Credit cards—MasterCard, Visa, and, to a much lesser extent, American Express and Diners Club—are accepted throughout South Africa and East Africa and at most group-owned lodges and hotels, but not much elsewhere. In Botswana, for instance, American Express cards are not accepted and Diners Club cards are rarely used. Always check in advance whether your preferred card is accepted at the lodge. If you're self-driving, note that many places prefer to be paid in the local currency, so make sure you change money where you can.

As a safety precaution, consider splitting up the way you carry your money: use your credit card for a third of your purchases, use traveler's checks for another third, and use cash for the remainder. Change traveler's checks when you can, in city banks and large hotels; many smaller towns and lodges don't accept traveler's checks.

TIP It's a good idea to notify your credit-card company that you will be traveling to Africa, so that the company doesn't deny transactions because of unusual usage patterns.

5

On Safari

You're in an open safari vehicle; the guide drives slowly and deliberately while the tracker scans the sandy ground to read the animal tracks from the night before. The tracker gives the guide a barely noticeable signal, a kind of shorthand developed over years of working together. Your eyes search and strain; anxiety rises. "Ingwe," the guide whispers, and the tracker nods almost imperceptibly. You're still trying to figure out what might be camouflaged in the thick tangle of riverine vegetation when suddenly a leopard breaks cover and darts across the road just a few yards from where you sit.

This is the heart of a safari and why you're going to Africa. Regardless of the safari destination you've chosen, all the areas have similarities: first, there's the overwhelming primeval atmosphere where you are the transient visitor in an ancient tableau of nature that has been going on since the dawn of time. Then there are the animals, from tiny rodents to the largest of land mammals, all going about their daily business of feeding, either killing or avoiding being killed, and the never-ending territorial disputes that have evolved between species to ensure the maximum reproductive success of each animal group. The species you see are selected by time and nature: they are supremely adapted to their unforgiving habitats. You can move through the scene in dreamlike wonderment, but the strong scents of the bush, the birdsong, the bellows, and the roars, will let you know you are very much awake, and alive.

GAME VIEWING

Until several decades ago, the Big Five—buffalo, elephants, leopards, lions, and rhinoceroses—were present in just about every game reserve. In many areas today, however, poaching and in some cases poor land management have brought about local extinction, mainly of elephants and rhinos. In the mid-1980s the Lower Zambezi Valley had 10,000 black rhinos, the highest concentration in the world. Today it has none. North Luangwa National Park, in Zambia, once had the largest elephant herds on the continent, but heavy poaching throughout the 1980s decimated their numbers.

Still, places remain where you can see all of the Big Five. If viewing big game, and especially the five "big ones," is your priority, your best options are the Serengeti National Park in Tanzania; the adjoining Masai Mara National Reserve, across the border in Kenya; or one of the lodges in the Sabi Sand private game reserve in South Africa. Some lodges in the Sabi Sand, such as Mala Mala, make their reputations on offering tours that show you the Big Five—and they even give you a certificate that says you've seen them all to prove it to your friends.

These places are among the most popular safari destinations and are usually the choice of first-time visitors to Africa. However, because of the large number of other safari goers in these locations, the experience often feels like more of a game-viewing tour than a safari. This is especially true of East African parks such as Tanzania's Serengeti and Kenya's Amboseli, where minibuses with pop-up roofs are used on game drives. Riding around in a bus is not everyone's idea of a great bush experience. But even these reserves include smaller bush camps away from the crowds, and these options aren't necessarily more expensive than the better-known large hotels and lodges. Good examples of such smaller operations are Grumeti River

Camp and Klein's Camp in the Serengeti's central Seronera plains.

Repeat visitors to Africa, feeling more confident about being in the bush than on previous trips, often choose more-adventurous safaris, such as walking or canoeing options. The trade-off is that the game spotting on these types of trips is more random; there are no Big Five guarantees; and every good sighting requires effort. Sometimes you're lucky enough to spot animals before you've spent much time looking for them. But there is a special satisfaction when you have a great sighting after hours of searching and following tracks.

TIP At most Southern African and some East African camps and lodges, open vehicles with raised, stepped seating—meaning the seats in back are higher than the ones in front—are used for game drives. There are usually three rows of seats after the driver's row; the norm at a luxury lodge is to have two people per row. In the front row you'll have the clearest conversations with the ranger, but farther back you'll have a clearer, elevated view over the front of the car. Whenever possible, avoid the back row; you're exposed to the most dust and feel the most bumps in these seats, and communicating with your ranger is difficult because of the rows between you. In closed vehicles, which are used in East Africa and by private touring companies operating in Kruger National Park, sit as close to the driver-guide as possible so you can get in and out of the vehicle more easily and get the best views.

Respecting Wildlife

Immersion in the pristine environment of African safari lands is a privilege. In order to preserve this privilege for future generations, it's important to view wildlife with minimal disturbance and to avoid upsetting the delicate balance of nature at all costs. Remember that you're a visitor to these animals' territories, so act like you would in someone else's home: respect their space.

Nature is neither kind nor sentimental. Nothing is wasted in the great pyramid of life in the African bush: from lion and hyena to vulture and jackal to dung beetle. Do not be tempted to interfere with these natural processes. The animals are going about the business of survival in a harsh environment, and you can unwittingly make their survival difficult. Don't get too close to the animals; you might cause alarm or influence a hunt by chasing away the prey or shielding a predator's approach. Don't even pick up a tortoise to help it across some perceived obstacle: you have no idea what it's really trying to do, or where it wants to go. If you're intrusive, you could drive animals away from feeding and, even worse, from drinking at water holes, where they are very skittish and vulnerable to predators. That time at the water hole may be their only opportunity to drink that day.

THE BIG FIVE IN SOUTHERN AFRICA

	ELEPHANT	LION
South Africa		
Kruger	Plentiful	Plentiful
Sabi Sand	Good	Plentiful
Kgalagadi	N/A	Good
Hluhluwe-Umfolozi	Plentiful	Good
Botswana		
Okavango Delta	Plentiful	Good
Moremi	Plentiful	Plentiful
Chobe	Plentiful	Plentiful
Namibia		
Etosha	Plentiful	Plentiful
Skeleton Coast	Good	Extinct
Zimbabwe		
Hwange	Plentiful	Plentiful
Kariba	Plentiful	Good
Mana Pools	Plentiful	Plentiful
Zambia		
South Luangwa	Plentiful	Plentiful
Kafue	Good	Good
Malawi		
Liwonde	Plentiful	Rare

BUFFALO	LEOPARD	W RHINO	B RHINO
Plentiful	Good	Good	Rare
Plentiful	Plentiful	Good	Rare
N/A	Good	N/A	N/A
Plentiful	Rare	Plentiful	Good
Plentiful	Good	Extinct/Reintroduced	Extinct
Plentiful	Plentiful	Extinct	Extinct
Good	Good	Extinct	Extinct
N/A	Rare	N/A	Good
N/A	Rare	N/A	Extinct
Plentiful	Good	Rare	Rare
Plentiful	Good	Extinct	Extinct/Reintroduced
Plentiful	Good	N/A	Extinct
Plentiful	Plentiful	Extinct	Extinct
Good	Rare	Extinct	Extinct
Rare	Rare	N/A	Extinct

OTHER ANIMALS IN SOUTHERN AFRICA

South Africa

Kruger and Sabi Sand	wild dog, cheetah, zebra, wildebeest, giraffe, kudu, impala, small antelope, raptors and other birds
Kgalagadi	oryx, cheetah, jackal, brown hyena, raptors, springbok, wildebeest, hartebeest, eland
Hluhluwe-Umfolozi	plains game, nyala, reedbuck, zebra, giraffe, kudu

Botswana

Okavango Delta	hippo, crocodile, impala, kudu, wild dog, sitatunga, lechwe, waterbirds
Moremi	sable and roan antelope, kudu, tsessebe, impala, wild dog, cheetah, hyena, zebra, giraffe
Chobe	puku, bushbuck, hyena, sable antelope, kudu

Namibia

Etosha	oryx, eland, roan antelope, flamingo, ostrich, wildebeest, zebra, springbok, Damara dik-dik, cheetah, jackal, black-faced impala
Skeleton Coast	desert elephant, seal, hyena and jackal, oryx, springbok, ostrich

Zimbabwe

Hwange	sable and roan antelope, impala, wild dog, hyena, serval, civet, giraffe, wildebeest, raptors, cheetah
Kariba	crocodile and hippo, sable and roan antelope, kudu, eland, bushbuck and waterbuck
Mana Pools	hyena, hippo, crocodile, waterbirds, kudu, nyala, zebra, eland

Zambia

South Luangwa	hippo, crocodile, sable and roan antelope, puku, eland, aquatic birds, Defassa waterbuck, Thornicroft's giraffe
Kafue	wild dog, sable and roan antelope, Defassa waterbuck, tsessebe, hartebeest, lechwe, puku, hippo, crocodile

Malawi

Liwonde	river birds, hippo, crocodile, sable antelope, waterbuck, bushbuck, impala

THE BIG FIVE IN EAST AFRICA

	ELEPHANT	LION
Kenya		
Masai Mara	Plentiful	Plentiful
Amboseli	Plentiful	Extinct
Tsavo	Plentiful	Plentiful
Samburu	Good	Good
Tanzania		
Serengeti	Plentiful	Plentiful
Ngorongoro	Plentiful	Plentiful
Selous	Plentiful	Plentiful
Uganda		
Murchison Falls	Good	Rare

OTHER ANIMALS IN EAST AFRICA

Kenya

Masai Mara	cheetah, Masai giraffe, wildebeest migration, crocodile, topi
Amboseli and Tsavo	flamingo, cheetah, hyena, gerenuk, hippo
Samburu	gerenuk, Somali ostrich, Grevy's zebra, reticulated giraffe, Beisa oryx, Reiney's gazelle, Kirk's and Geunther's dik-dik, eland

BUFFALO	LEOPARD	W RHINO	B RHINO
Plentiful	Plentiful	Extinct	Good
Plentiful	Rare	N/A	N/A
Plentiful	Good	N/A	Rare/Reintroduced
Good	Rare	N/A	N/A
Plentiful	Plentiful	Good	Good
Plentiful	Rare	N/A	Good
Plentiful	Plentiful	N/A	Rare
Good	Rare	Extinct	Extinct

Tanzania	
Serengeti	cheetah, wildebeest, zebra, topi, kongoni, eland, giraffe
Ngorongoro	flamingo, kongoni, eland, hyena
Selous	crocodile, hippo, aquatic birds, Selous wildebeest, eland, greater kudu, giraffe, Lichtenstein's hartebeest
Uganda	
Murchison Falls	shoebill stork, hippo, huge crocodile, aquatic birds, Uganda kob, Jackson's hartebeest

☐ **Extinct:** no longer in existence on a local level

☐ **Good:** means there have been widespread sightings in the area and you have a better-than-average chance of seeing this animal

☐ **Plentiful:** the chance of seeing this animal is excellent

☐ **Rare:** the species is seldom seen but may exist in close range

☐ **Reintroduced:** the animal is being brought back to the area in small numbers but in some instances may be confined to a pro-tected, fenced space

The black rhinoceros and the white rhinoceros are distinct species so they are sepa-rated on the charts. The black rhino is smaller, more aggressive, and stays in dense bush areas; the white rhino is larger, less aggressive, and grazes in open grasslands.

Never feed any wild creature—not a cute monkey, not an inquisitive baboon, not a baby tree squirrel, or a young bird out of its nest. When you feed wild ani-mals, you help to habituate them to humans, and the animals get closer to humans than they normally would. If an animal then feels threatened, the likeli-hood of a fatal attack increases. Feeding young birds can transfer your scent to them or to their nest. In either case you are ultimately signing the animal's death warrant because problem animals will eventually have to be shot and adult birds will abandon their young if they smell of humans. Also, by giving food you diminish that animal's ability to feed itself. In some cases, such as where lodges throw their waste into the veld, baboons and other animals can become displaced like city tramps.

In some camps and lodges animals have gotten used to being fed or stealing food. The most common animals in this category are baboons and monkeys; in some places they sneak into huts, tents, and even occupied vehicles to snatch food. If you see primates around, keep all food out of sight, and keep your windows rolled up. (If a baboon manages to get into your vehicle, he will trash the interior as he searches for food and pretty much use your car as a bathroom.) Otherwise, give them a wide berth—even vacate an area if they seem intent on being there. Like other animals, baboons and monkeys are vicious when they feel threatened or cornered, and they have huge canine teeth. A male baboon can kill a leopard, and a monkey will easily overpower you and deliver nasty wounds.

DRIVING DIRECTIONS Although most animals in popular parks are accustomed to vehicles with humans in them and will carry on unperturbed in many cases, a vehicle should still approach any animal cautiously and quietly, and the driver should "feel" the response. As soon as an effect is noted he should slow down or stop, depending on the circumstances. Human presence among wild animals never goes unnoticed. In the Serengeti and Masai Mara, cheetah survival is being jeopardized by guides who try to drive too close to them, thereby giving up the cheetah's location to its prey or sometimes just chasing away the skittish cat, thus impacting the animal's ability to hunt, eat, and ultimately survive.

Even if you're not at the wheel, you should try to gauge when your presence begins to have an effect on the animals and then stop—despite the urge to get as close as you can. Not all game guides and rangers are sensitive to this, their focus being on giving you the best sighting. But if you feel uncomfortable, say so.

When self-driving in a game area, err on the side of caution by always approaching animals slowly for your own and the animals' safety. A careful, quiet approach also gives you a better chance of getting as close as possible without alarming the animal. Don't get out of the vehicle, even if the animals appear friendly, and don't feed the creatures. Animals don't associate people in a vehicle with the potential food source or possible threat that they are when out of the vehicle. But for this ruse to work you must be quiet and still. The smell of the exhaust fumes and noise of a vehicle mask the presence of the human cargo, so when the engine is off you need to exercise extra caution. This is especially true when closely viewing lions and elephants—the only two animals likely to attack a vehicle or people in a vehicle. When approaching lions or elephants, never leap out of your seat or talk loudly; you want to be able to get as close as possible without scaring them off, and you want to avoid provoking an attack.

GAME-WATCHING DO'S & DON'TS

► Observe animals silently and with a minimum of disturbance to their natural activities. Standing up in your vehicle and talking loudly on game drives can frighten animals away.

► Never attempt to attract an animal's attention. Don't imitate animal sounds, clap your hands, pound the vehicle, or throw objects.

► Show respect for your driver and guide's judgment: don't insist that he take the vehicle closer so you can get a better photograph. Getting too close may hinder a hunt or cause animals to abandon a hard-earned meal and put you in danger. Driving off-road in certain areas can cause the guide to lose his license.

► Don't litter—any tossed item can choke or poison animals and birds.

► Never attempt to feed or approach any wild animal. This is especially important to remember near lodges and in campgrounds where animals may have become accustomed to human visitors.

► Refrain from smoking on game drives. The dry African bush ignites easily.

► Dress in neutral-tone clothes because animals pay the least attention to muted colors; if everyone in the car is wearing beige, brown, green, and tan, the animal sees one large vegetation-colored mass.

► Use a minimum of body fragrances for the benefit of both the animals and your fellow travelers.

AN ANIMAL-SURVIVAL GUIDE

On an organized safari where you are in the care of a professional guide or ranger, you're unlikely to be placed in a dangerous situation. If you're going for a walk, ride, or paddle in dangerous territory, your guide will first brief you about all the possible dangers and tell you how to behave in the unlikely event of an emergency. Listen to all the safety briefings and adhere to them strictly.

Never try to get an animal to pose with you. This is probably the biggest cause of death and injury on safaris, when visitors don't listen to or believe the warnings from their rangers or posted notices in the public parks. The animals are not cute and they are not tame. An herbivore impala, giraffe, or ostrich can kill you just as easily as a lion, elephant, or buffalo can. Smaller animals such as mongooses and otters are also predators that can kill or injure something much bigger than themselves, so stay clear of them as well.

Other animals may not be such active and aggressive pests, but pose problems of their own. The honey badger, for example, is an intriguing animal. It's black and white, looks like a skunk on steroids, and walks with the swaying gait of a large lizard. Although the honey badger is the size of a small dog, it's one of the fiercest animals in Africa and will stand up to a large lion. If you see one around, give it a wide berth—most people in the know would rather face just about any other animal than an enraged honey badger.

Caution is your most trusted safety measure. Keep your distance, and keep your hands to yourself, and you should be fine. However, here are some worst-case-scenario survival tips to use if you ever find yourself alone in the bush.

AFRICAN BUFFALO Often referred to as Cape buffalo, these are not to be confused with Asian water buffalo or, for that matter, with North American bison. This is an altogether heftier and more dangerous animal and should not be approached. Buffalo in a herd are seldom any problem because their best defense is to present a solid wall of horns to an enemy. The real dangers are the lone old males that have been kicked out of the herd and skulk along river courses in the dense bush or reeds. These buffalo are called dagha boys; dagha is the clay mixture used for building huts, and these old guys spend much of their days in mud wallows and are usually thickly coated in the stuff. If a buffalo charges you, run for the nearest cover. If it is too close, you must try to leap out of the way of its slashing horns. If it is upon you, your best bet is to lie flat on the ground; it will try to butt and gore you, but you can minimize the damage by playing dead.

ELEPHANTS Although usually placid creatures, the exception is female elephants with their young—always keep your distance from breeding herds. When an elephant trumpets in a showy manner, head held up and ears spread wide, it's a mock display or mock charge—terrifying to witness up close but not physically dangerous. If an elephant stamps the ground, puts its ears back and its head forward, and issues a loud, high-pitched screech, you're in for real trouble. Your only option is flight, very quick flight—a charging elephant is extremely fast and surprisingly agile. If you're in open ground, make for the nearest big tree, ditch, or embankment; elephants will seldom attempt to negotiate these obstacles. If there really is no chance of making cover, then try to find sticks to throw—anything to break the elephant's stride and give you a few crucial seconds to make an escape. If you're in a vehicle, leave the area quickly.

HIPPOPOTAMUSES Although they may be comical looking, these are actually one of Africa's most dangerous animals. They are fanatically territorial, and if you wander into their space, they will most likely confront you. The most common threat display is the yawn; no, it's not tired, it's telling you to back off. Hippos, like elephants, often mock charge, but it's not easy to tell a mock from the real thing until it's too late. When approaching hippos in the water, rap your paddle on your boat to alert them of your approach, and give them a wide berth. If hippos block the entire channel, as they can do in the Zambezi and Luangwa rivers, then head for the bank. Wait to see if they give way, or consider portaging around them. Never get between a hippo and the main river channels, as this will appear to them that you're trying to corner them and may result in an attack. On land, hippos are most aggressive if you get between them and the water when they're trying to return after an evening of grazing. Unfortunately, the people who suffer most from this type of attack are poor locals without running water who need to use the river as a water source and often end up directly in a hippo's path. Although you cannot outpace a hippo on land, less so in the water, it is the slowest of the big animals, and if you have a reasonably large head start, you have a chance of reaching cover before it closes the gap.

HYENA Although not usually thought of as a threat to humans, hyenas scavenge at night, and there are horror stories of hyenas sneaking into unclosed tents, even pushing open hut doors, and killing people in their sleep. This happens extremely rarely, and if you are cautious it won't happen to you. The biggest myth about hyenas is that they are not good hunters. The truth is that they are almost always more successful hunters than are lions in the same areas. If you see a battle or standoff between lions and hyenas over a carcass, chances are that the hyenas made the kill and the lions moved in and chased them off. In the unlikely event of a hyena attack, your best defense is to go ballistic: make as loud a noise and as much movement as you can, and use anything that comes to hand as a weapon. A lone hyena is an opportunist and, when confronted, will take flight rather than fight.

LEOPARDS These are very secretive animals and there are few cases of their confronting humans other than hunters. Any attack will be swift and silent so there will be little time for reaction or flight. If you do see a leopard you should back away without turning or running. Although lions rely on their massive jaws and canine teeth to do damage, leopards use a combination of teeth and razor-sharp claws. As with any large predator, if you aren't armed your best defense is to make as big and noisy a display as you can to confuse the animal and halt its attack. Just one moment's confusion will usually give you the chance to face it off and back away.

LIONS They are called the king of beasts for good reason. Although they sleep for up to 18 hours a day and can seem like the laziest of animals, that is their royal prerogative. When lions move, they can do so with awesome speed and power. A charging lion can cover 330 feet in four seconds. Male lions can bring down adult giraffes, buffalo, hippos, even small elephants.

Stories of hunters surviving lion attacks are numerous; tales of hunters killing lions in close combat are more rare. Remember: if faced by an angry lion, do not turn or run. A lion considers any moving animal prey and will instinctively attack; you cannot begin to think of outpacing a charging lion. A flicking tail is your first sign that the animal is angry and is considering an attack: this is the time to carefully back away toward cover. If a lion is coming at you, stand your ground, shout or scream as loudly as you can, and even wave your arms and try to be menacing, if only to confuse and stop it for a moment. If the lion stops, look in its direction but don't stare directly into its eyes, as that will be seen as a challenge; then slowly back away, always facing it. If the lion comes again, use whatever is at hand to throw at it, shouting all the time. Never,

ever turn your back to a lion and try to run—that is your death warrant. If an attack presses on, your best bet is to "play dead" and to protect your neck with an arm or stick to prevent a paralyzing bite.

NILE CROCODILES Despite their deadly reputation and fearsome looks, these are shy creatures; it's just that they have to eat sometimes. When they're really big, almost anything that moves is on the menu. If you go to places such as the Lower Zambezi, Masai Mara, Selous, South Luangwa, and Murchison Falls, you're going to see them in great numbers—and of great size. You need to take heed of them if you're on a canoe safari, as suddenly you're on their turf. The other danger spots are camping on the shore of any large river, or swimming in the Okavango Delta, even at traditional swimming spots; the golden rule is that crocodiles are everywhere, so don't chance a swim in suspect waters.

In most cases as you approach a basking croc it will either stay absolutely still, or it will slide off into the water and you won't see it again. If a crocodile grabs you when you're swimming, the best thing to do is fight. Reptiles don't chew but instead rip and swallow. You have to prevent it from getting such a good grip on any part of your body that it can start twisting you around. It will often let go to get a better grip, and that is your chance to move and counterattack. The most successful defense is to actually thrust your arm right down the crocodile's throat: it has a flap to stop taking in water and if you can open it, it will have to let go.

ON HUNTING THE BIG FIVE

The chase of the elephant, if persistently followed, entails more fatigue and hardship than any other kind of African hunting. As regards risk, it is hard to say whether it is more or less dangerous than the chase of the lion or the buffalo. Both Cuninghame and Tarlton, men of wide experience, ranked elephant-hunting, in point of danger, as nearly on the level with lion-hunting, and more dangerous than buffalo-hunting; all three kinds are far more dangerous than the chase of the rhino. Personally, I believe the actual conflict with a lion, where the conditions are the same, to be normally the more dangerous sport, though far greater demands are made by elephant-hunting on the qualities of personal endurance and hardihood and resolute perseverance in the face of disappointment and difficulty. Buffalo seemingly do not charge as freely as elephant, but are more dangerous when they do charge. Rhino, when hunted, though at times ugly customers, seem to me certainly less dangerous than the other three; but from sheer stupid truculence they are themselves apt to take the offensive in unexpected fashion, being far more prone to such aggression than any of the others—man-eating lions always excepted . . . Not even in Africa is there a beast of more unflinching courage than the spotted cat. The leopard is smaller than any full-grown male cougar I have ever killed, and yet cougars often kill game rather heavier

> than leopards usually venture upon;
> yet very few cougars indeed show
> anything like the pluck and ferocity
> shown by [this] leopard, characteristic
> of its kind.

– from African Game Trails
by Theodore Roosevelt

But you're going to get a sore arm in the process. Other than that, go for the eyes with anything you have, or try to grab around its body so it cannot bite you, and scream for help.

RHINOCEROSES Massive, primeval-looking animals, they are potentially very dangerous. Their eyesight is relatively poor, but not nearly as bad as some people think. The natural response of a rhinoceros is to charge anything it deems threatening. The black, or hook-lipped, species is more aggressive than the larger white, or square-lipped, rhino. Both types of rhinos charge hard and fast with their horn held low, to be used as a sword or battering ram. If you can leap out of the way of the scything horn, the rhinos will in most cases carry on straight, and seldom turn around to charge again. All the same, if you have escaped the first charge, run as quickly as your legs permit for cover—any cover, including a rock or bush, but preferably a large tree, even a thorn tree.

OTHER SAFETY TIPS At night, never sleep out in the open in any area with wildlife. If you're sleeping in a tent make sure it's fully closed; if it's a small tent, place something between you and the side of the wall to prevent an opportunistic bite from the outside. If you're in your tent and not exposed, you should be quite safe. Few people lose their lives to lions or hyenas. Malaria is a much more real danger, so keep your tent zipped up tight at night to keep out mosquitoes.

Nearly all camps and lodges insist that an armed ranger accompany you at night; no one should ever walk without an armed chaperone at night. If, for some inexplicable reason, you are walking alone, you should carry and use a flashlight—known locally as a torch—which all lodges and even tented camps supply. Shine your torch in a wide arc all around you; if there's anything lurking up ahead you'll see its eyes shining. If you do pick up any night eyes, back off slowly in the direction you came from and call a ranger to accompany you. If you find yourself isolated and feel threatened, make a noise. But don't turn around and run; if it's a predator, it will pounce on you. If you hear the thumping footfalls of a large beast—hippopotamus, elephant, buffalo, or rhinoceros—jump off the path and out of its way. Small nocturnal creatures such as owls and bush babies have large eyes that, when caught in the light, may make you think they belong to a huge monster. Go call a ranger or member of the camp staff; it's always better to err on the side of safety.

TIP If you're walking in the bush at night, whistle or sing to alert anything or anyone in your path. The biggest danger is that you will startle an animal by suddenly bearing down on it; it will attack as its first means of defense.

GAME RANGERS & TRACKERS

Game rangers (sometimes referred to as guides) tend to be of two types: those who have come to conservation by way of hunting and those who are professional conservationists. In both cases they have vast experience with and knowledge of the bush and the animals that inhabit it. Tourism and the advent of photographic safaris have led to new professional opportunities for these highly trained people, and you can take both pleasure and comfort in their company.

A ranger's job on safari is multifaceted: to entertain you, protect you, and put you as close to the wilderness as possible while serving as bush mechanic, first-aid specialist, and host. This is no small feat, and each ranger has his particular strengths. Because of the intensity of the safari experience, with its exposure to potentially dangerous animals and tricky situations, your relationship with your guide or ranger is a unique one of trust, friendliness, and respect. Misunderstandings may sometimes occur, but you're one step closer to ensuring that all goes well if you know the protocols and expectations.

Rangers work in conjunction with trackers, who sit in a special seat on the front of the four-wheel-drive vehicle, spot animals, and guide the rangers on where to go. If the tracker speaks good English and seems comfortable talking to you, consider discussing animals with him.

HOW SHOULD I TREAT MY RANGER OR GUIDE?

Acknowledge that the guide is a professional and an expert in the field, and defer to his knowledge. Instead of trying to show how much you know, follow the example of the hunter, which is to walk quietly and take notice of all little signs around you. Save social chatter with the guide for when you're back at camp, not out on a game drive. Rangers appreciate questions, which give them an idea of your range of knowledge and of how much detail to include in their animal descriptions. However, if you like to ask a lot of questions, save some for later, especially as several other people are likely to be in the safari vehicle with you. Carry a pocket notebook on game drives and jot down questions as they occur; you can then bring them up at dinner or around the campfire, when your ranger has more time to talk and everyone can participate in the discussion.

HOW SHOULD MY RANGER TREAT ME?

You can expect your ranger or guide to treat you with respect: you are the client and he is the service provider, and you can expect delivery of that service 100% of the time. A guide should be pleasant and friendly but never too chummy or, worse, patronizing. If you believe a show-off guide or gung-ho ranger is speaking down to you, a quiet word with him should be enough to change his demeanor. (The safari world is small; a guide's reputation is built by word of mouth and can be eroded in the same fashion.)

Don't let your ranger get away with rote guiding, or "guiding by numbers," whereby he provides only a list of an animal's attributes. Push him by asking questions and showing you want, and expect, more. Even the best guides may experience "bush burnout" by the end of a busy safari season with demanding clients, but any guide worthy of the title always goes out of his way to give you the best possible experience. If you suspect yours has a case of burnout, or just laziness, you have a right to ask for certain things to be done. There's never any harm in asking, and you can't expect your guide to read your mind about what you like. If, for example, you have a preference for birds, insects, or whatever, ask your guide to spend time on these subjects. You may be surprised by how happy he is oblige.

TIP Gratuities are a fact of life on safari. In Southern Africa you may tip in U.S. currency or in rand; in East Africa, tips may be paid in U.S. dollars or in the local currency. It's customary for rangers to receive US\$5 to US\$10 per day per traveler; trackers usually get US\$3 to US\$5 per day. Tips are presented as a lump sum at the end of the trip; consider including a thank-you note with the tip as a personal touch. For general staff, US\$5 after a two- or three-day stay is sufficient.

HEALTH ON SAFARI

Dehydration & Overheating

Of all the horror stories and fantastic nightmares about meeting your end in the bush—being devoured by lions and crocodiles; succumbing to some ghastly fever, like Ernest Hemingway's hero in *The Snows of Kilimanjaro;* facing a party of spear-thrusting Masai— the problem you're most likely to encounter will be of your own doing: dehydration.

The African sun is hot and the air is dry, and sweat evaporates quickly in these conditions. You might not realize how much bodily fluid you are losing as a result. Wear a hat, lightweight clothing, and sunscreen— all of which will help your body cope with high temperatures.

Drink at least two to three quarts of water a day, and in extreme heat conditions as much as three to four quarts of water or juice. Drink more if you're exerting yourself physically. If you overdo it at dinner with wine or spirits or even caffeine, you need to drink even more water. Anti-malarial medications are also very dehydrating, so it's important to increase your water intake while you're taking this medicine.

Don't rely on thirst to tell you when to drink; people often don't feel thirsty until they're a little dehydrated. At the first sign of dry mouth, exhaustion, or headache, drink water because dehydration is the likely culprit. To test for dehydration, pinch the skin on the back of

A COMMON SAFARI AFFLICTION

"Khaki fever" is a safari disease as well known as malaria. It was part of the plot-line in the film *Mogambo,* in which the married society girl (Grace Kelly) falls for the rugged, tanned game ranger (Clark Gable), who's already carrying on with a wild American (Ava Gardner).

You're on safari, a magical world quite unlike the one to which you're accustomed, and in a good mood; romantic notions fill your head, and here's this tanned, knowledgeable ranger protecting you from the wilds of Africa, chauffeuring you around, and seemingly delivering your every wish. Or: your ranger has been in the bush for months and has become a little overly cocky thanks to all the attractive clients he or she has been coddling during the season (in reality the majority of rangers are men; female rangers, though they do exist, are few and far between). The campfire is seductive and the bush is full of bewitching, sensual stimuli—a full moon hovers above the trees, a lion roars in the distance, a nightjar fills the velvety night with its trilling call. Heavenly things happen. If they do, just make sure you are prepared for the earthbound realities. AIDS in Africa is rife; if there's even the remotest chance of having a sexual encounter on safari, carry condoms. Khaki fever is widespread, so don't expect this to be a match made in the heavens.

your hand and see if it stays in a peak; if it does, you're dehydrated. Drink a solution of ½ teaspoon of salt and 4 tablespoons of sugar dissolved in a quart of water to replace electrolytes. Advanced dehydration can lead to heat cramps, heat exhaustion, or the more-serious heatstroke.

Heat cramps usually occur in the abdomen, arms, or legs. When these occur, stop all activity and sit quietly in a cool spot and drink. If cramps persist for more than an hour, seek medical assistance.

Signs of heat exhaustion include headache, nausea, pale and clammy skin, profuse sweating, and weakness or dizziness. Fever of above 104°F is the main sign of heatstroke, or sunstroke. A rapid pulse, fainting, confusion, shallow breathing, and hot red skin are other symptoms of this life-threatening condition. In either case the first goal is to lower the person's temperature, via fanning, cold compresses or ice packs, or a cool bath. Seek medical help as soon as possible.

TIP Sleeping under a mosquito net or in an insect-proof tent is customary, but it can stifle airflow. If you can't sleep, wet a sheet, wring it out, and lie under it: you'll fall asleep before you know it.

Food for Thought

Like learning to speak a bit of the local language, you get a better sense of a country if you at least try the local food. Fresh mopane worms, quick-fried termites, and rat kebabs are the absolute extremes of African cooking and probably won't be on a safari-camp menu, but local dishes such as ostrich meat, crocodile, or springbok (a type of venison) likely will be offered and are definitely worth trying. Expect also to see African staples such as corn on the cob, *pap* (a type of cornmeal), and *peri-peri* (hot-pepper sauce) at the safari table.

At many lodges, food is considered an expression of the property's style and service, and even on the least-expensive safari you dine on wonderfully fresh and abundant meats, salads, vegetables, and fruits, lots of starchy foods—potatoes, pastas, biscuits, freshly baked bread—and dessert. So you're not going to lose weight on safari, but are in fact in danger of putting it on unless you're hiking or paddling every day. If the menu is going to be an issue for you, take small portions and eat with discretion. If you have a problem with weight control, you should ask the lodge manager about getting sensible, low-carbohydrate meals or servings. Inform your travel agent or tour operator of any dietary restrictions you have—vegetarian or vegan diet, lactose intolerance—when you book your safari. Camp kitchens often order food months in advance, so the more time they have to plan for your special needs the better.

TIP Fresh produce and ordinary tap water are generally safe in South Africa, Botswana, Namibia, and Zimbabwe, but elsewhere, unless you're in a luxury hotel or lodge, you need to drink bottled water and eat according to the traveler's code—boil it, cook it, peel it, or forget it.

Malaria

The disease is spread by the female Anopheles mosquito, which is infected with the malaria parasite and operates between dawn and dusk. These pests can develop resistance to anti-malarial drugs, so even if you're taking the newest drug, take great care to avoid mosquito bites.

Wear clothes you've treated with a mosquito-repellent spray or laundry wash (see Chapter 4 for additional information), especially in the morning and evening, when you should tuck your pants into your socks. Wearing light-color clothing while on safari helps to deter mosquitoes (as well as tsetse flies), which are attracted to dark surfaces. Spray all exposed skin with a mosquito-repellent spray that contains DEET, unless you're pregnant or nursing. DEET isn't recommended for children. Citronella and other natural bug repellents are options, but they're not as potent, so vigilance is crucial.

Mosquitoes can't fly well in moving air, so if your room has a fan over or facing your bed, keep it on while you sleep. Use mosquito coils and sprays in your room (especially if you're traveling with children), and sleep under mosquito nets. Mosquito nets shouldn't have holes or gaps and can be treated in permethrin, which is the active ingredient found in mosquito-repellent spray and laundry wash and may be sold as Permanone and Duranon.

If you have been infected, you won't feel the effects until 7 to 90 days afterward. Symptoms mimic those of the flu, with escalating high fever, shivers and sweating, headache, and muscle aches. If you feel ill even several months after your trip, be sure to tell your doctor that you have been in a malaria-infected area.

Motion Sickness

If you're prone to motion sickness, be sure to examine your safari itinerary closely. Choose safari camps that have easy access by chartered planes on paved landing strips. If you're going on safari to northern Botswana (the Okavango Delta, specifically) and Tanzania's "southern circuit" (Selous and Ruaha game reserves), know that small planes and unpaved airstrips are the main means of transportation between camps; these trips can be very bumpy, hot, and a little dizzying even if you're not prone to motion sickness. The first preventive is not to go on a safari that involves flying in small planes. If, however, you've set your heart on a trip to one of these areas, try to book an itinerary in which your transfers are done in early morning or late afternoon. Not only is the light softer, but the air is more stable, and the temperatures are cooler. If you fly between midmorning and midafternoon, expect a bumpy ride as the small plane hits rising thermal pockets in the hot afternoon air.

TIP When you fly in small planes take a sun hat and a pair of sunglasses: if you sit in the front seat next to the pilot, or on the side of the sun, you will experience harsh glare that could give you a severe headache and exacerbate motion sickness.

6

More About Africa

The cultural landscape of Southern and East Africa is a complex tapestry woven from layers of language and tradition. It includes diminutive Bushmen hunter-gatherers, regal Masai herders, and Dutch farmers. Beyond the largest cities, Africa is still heavily tribal, and modern attitudes can easily be out of place—even offensive. In traditional African society, behavior is usually dignified and respectful; if you learn some basic customs, such as how to hand something over to or accept something from someone, you will be treated more courteously in return.

LOCAL CULTURE & CUSTOMS

An African will never ask a stranger directly for something without at least first saying "hello" and passing some pleasantries. To walk up to someone and say, "I would like a Coke" or "Which is the way to Harare?" is considered rude and will invariably evoke a sullen response. "Hello" and "how are you" are the basic starting points of any conversation. However, the basis of African culture is built on the passing of news, so you really are expected to give more information—who you are, where you've come from, where you're going, and what the weather was like where you were last. Shaking hands is also a universal African custom: not the firm, businesslike shake used in the West, but a friendly, touching clasp that can make some Westerners feel edgy.

Most African people give and receive items with their right hand; the left hand is held open under the right forearm. This gesture is as important to them as placing your hand in front of your mouth when you cough or sneeze. The origin of this custom was to show you weren't concealing a weapon, but now it's just a sign of good manners.

In black rural areas in Southern Africa, the height of bad manners is to sit on the bare ground; you should make a point of sitting on something, anything, such as a hat, jacket, newspaper, or handkerchief. When entering a *kraal* (traditional home), men should sit on the right-hand side and women on the left. The origin of this custom was protection in the event of attack; the men's spear arms were ready to turn into the oncoming danger.

Even though many African homesteads have rudimentary doors, never enter an African abode without announcing your arrival and gaining permission to enter, much as you knock on the door of a stranger's house.

Almost all African cultures are very conservative and male-dominated. By custom African women usually wait to be greeted by their "superiors," usually men. Don't go on safari with a missionary zeal to change these customs in two weeks, as you will likely leave a trail of resentment in your wake.

Officials in Africa

You need to know two important things about dealing with officials in Africa: first, people in uniforms take their elevated status seriously; and second, officials generally have all the time in the world, even though you may not. You cannot hope to win a tussle between yourself and an official, so don't act officious—no matter how right you think you are and how wrong you think they are. The best policy is to be friendly. Nine times out of 10 an African official will respond favorably to an overture of friendship.

Unfortunately, it's true that customs officials, police, and army personnel at roadblocks, and even staff at park entrances, may try to wheedle *baksheesh* (Aramaic for "bribe") out of you. The reason this tradition is widespread has less to do with hostility toward you

TIME ZONES

East Africa local time is three hours ahead of Greenwich Mean Time (GMT). That makes it eight hours ahead of Eastern Standard Time (EST; seven hours ahead during daylight saving time). Southern Africa operates on Central African Standard Time (CAST), which is two hours ahead of GMT, or seven hours ahead of EST (six hours ahead during daylight saving time). Namibia, however, seasonally uses something called Winter Time, one hour behind CAST, from 2 AM on the first Sunday of April until 2 AM on the first Sunday of September.

and more to do with how little these people are paid; often officials aren't paid for months on end and have to continue in their duties by stoicism and their wits.

The best, easiest, and cheapest way to handle this situation is to offer the person a small gift, such as a cigarette, a sweet, or a cold drink. The mere act of your giving and their accepting makes them indebted to you, and only the most churlish or desperate official will push for anything more.

When in airport lines, be prepared for long delays, and remember that you have to bide your time and wait your turn. When you reach the customs or immigration official, greet him nicely, in his own language if you can, and ask some basic information; an empathetic "Busy day?" might further ease your passage.

Make sure you approach a customs post or roadblock in a very unhurried manner or you may be there longer than you anticipated. Never try to rush an official or you might find yourself part of the "hurry up and wait" syndrome. If you feel you've been abused beyond any acceptable point, try to use psychology rather than confrontation: "Don't you need to get home today?" or "Are people in this country always so rude/unhelpful to visitors as this?" would be about as far as you'd want to go, playing on the African custom of treating visitors with respect and kindness.

Wealth & Poverty

Most of sub-Saharan Africa is considered poor, but there's a difference between a refugee or unemployed person in a city and a cattle herder in the outback. In the latter case the person is self-sufficient and doesn't want your sympathy or your charity. The former does, however. The point to remember is that wealth and poverty are relative. In Africa poor means no social security at all and not knowing where the next meal is coming from; it's about having nothing. However, that doesn't mean you should feel the need to put money in everyone's hands. By touring Africa, you're supporting local industry.

To help alleviate poverty in Africa, ensure that the safari company you use to handle your travel arrangements and the camps and lodges where you stay are all practicing sustainable tourism by supporting conservation and the enrichment of local communities. These measures might include providing employment to locals as well as contributing to local schools, water-purification plants, medical clinics, and other self-help projects. Support of this nature can have an incredible trickle-down effect within a community and will undoubtedly go a lot further than your handing out charity to one or two individuals. Talk to your travel agent or tour operator if you wish to make a donation toward any such project.

TIP Rather than handing out money, take along pens, pencils, and notepads to give out in rural areas, where many schools lack the most basic supplies.

SAFETY

Safari areas—relatively remote areas for the most part accessible to a limited number of staff and guests—are some of the safest places in the world. Lodges out in the wild are usually safe from petty crime. Small-time pilfering or theft are more likely to occur in bigger and more centrally located lodges, where greater numbers of people can access the camps.

Once you leave the remote safari areas and enter the cities and towns, take some basic safety precautions. First, keep in mind that some city areas are more dangerous than others. Areas to avoid if you're concerned about personal safety are primarily downtown Johannesburg and central Nairobi. In general, it's best to avoid deserted downtown areas after dark.

It's also a good idea to familiarize yourself with local customs before you go so that you don't offend locals and draw negative attention to yourself. For example, most of coastal East Africa is Muslim, so cover up appropriately if you plan to be in public Muslim areas. Also, try not to wear Bermuda shorts, brightly colored shirts, and socks with sandals—they usually mark you as a tourist.

SHOPPING

When bartering for souvenirs, food, or anything else, remember that there are two economies: one for locals and one for more affluent foreigners. Bartering and haggling over prices is the norm: you will often be quoted the top, outrageous price first, because there's a chance that you'll fall for it. On the other hand, don't necessarily assume you're being ripped off; it's just that bargaining is expected.

Before you start spending, try to establish the local price for, say, a taxi ride, a meal, and some souvenirs. You might still end up paying double, but not 10 times the local price you might be quoted. In just about every case, if you act and talk like an American, people will try to squeeze the maximum from you. In general, they do it because they're poor and often have plenty of mouths to feed, but it's also mostly because they can.

Although haggling over prices is customary, bear in mind that you can take bargaining too far and end up insulting the seller and making him go home short.

SAFETY TIPS FOR URBAN AREAS

▶ Leave expensive jewelry and valuables
  at home.

▶ Dress inconspicuously and modestly.

▶ Keep cameras and video cameras out
  of sight.

▶ Lock money and documents in a hotel
  safe.

▶ Watch for sneaky fingers in a crowd;
  keep your hands in your pockets if there's
  anything of value in them.

▶ Before you leave your hotel room, study
  your map and figure out exactly where
  you're going: there's no easier target than
  someone who's lost and bewildered.

▶ Don't be afraid to go out and sample local
  sights and culture—why else are you traveling? But go in a group, or get a taxi to
  take you to and collect you from a recommended place.

Start by offering one-third to one-half of the price
you're quoted and then feel your way up from there.
People are usually much more interested in making a
sale than ripping you off. In general you've done well if
you get away with paying two-thirds of the quoted
price; anything less than that and you've gotten a real
bargain.

In places such as the informal curio (souvenir or trin-
ket) markets in Dar es Salaam, the central craft market

in Nairobi, and markets around Victoria Falls, you could become quite intimidated by the throng that surrounds you, urging you to buy. This is one unfortunate aspect of traveling in the third world. If you have a guide he should ease you through these transactions and negotiate on your behalf, but even sometimes-noisome street touts can be your ally.

If you don't shop with a personal guide, remember never to give a curio "broker" or other hawker money on the promise that he'll return with something for you. There are probably more honest people than dishonest, but it's the dishonest ones who are looking for suckers, and this is one of the oldest tricks up their sleeves.

TIP In busy markets there's just too much competition for anyone to seriously overcharge, but don't make a purchase in the first five minutes. Walk around and try to get a feel for not only the prices but also the general vibe of the place. Don't start shopping until you feel you're in sync with it.

Buyer Beware

You will, undoubtedly, see things for sale in your travels that are made from endangered animals, especially if you spend time in Nairobi. These may include leopard skins, such horrors as elephant-foot stools and ashtrays, even gorilla hands and heads. Even if you are momentarily tempted to buy something made from an endangered species, know that you won't be able to get it back home. The United States prohibits the impor-

WHAT TO BUY

In each country, certain crafts and curios stand out. Listed below are some of the bargains and special items that might interest you.

- [ ] **Botswana:** grass baskets, bushman curios around Ghanzi

- [ ] **Kenya:** game trophies, Makonde wood carvings, jewelry with semiprecious stones, stone artifacts, sisal baskets

- [ ] **Malawi:** wood crafts, carved trinkets, wooden chief's chairs, baskets, pottery

- [ ] **Namibia:** game curios, gems and crystals, Ovambo wood carvings, bushman curios

- [ ] **South Africa:** gold jewelry, diamonds, wine, wildlife books and videos

- [ ] **Tanzania:** traditional African curios, Makonde carvings, musical instruments, Tingatinga paintings, batiks, soapstone and malachite knickknacks

- [ ] **Uganda:** large drums (other souvenirs are largely copied or imported from Kenya and Tanzania)

- [ ] **Zambia:** wood crafts, traditional curios

- [ ] **Zimbabwe:** stone carvings, wood carvings, traditional curios, pottery

tation of any item made from any endangered species, and the majority of other Western countries have similar prohibitions (most based on the rules set forth in the 1977 Convention on International Trade on Endangered Species).

In most cases you won't be able to bring elephant ivory into a Western country either. Views about ivory are mixed. Southern African states have been arguing for the right to trade their legal stockpiles of ivory from culled animals to help fund conservation; the East African countries hold that continued trade will fuel poaching and lead to local extinctions. The U.S. stance is clear, however: the African Elephant Conservation Act prohibits the import of ivory pieces into the United States unless they're antique and have documentation proving that they are more than 100 years old.

You should also abstain from purchasing large wood statues that represent an entire hardwood-forest tree. You may come across such items in Malawi and Zambia, two of the countries that specialize in wood carvings. Although craftspeople earn a living by selling these and other carvings, the sale of such large pieces increases the demand for wood, which in turn leads to the destruction of forests and eventually, perhaps, a community's ruin.

LOCAL WORDS & PHRASES

African countries are far less homogenous in language than most North American or European countries. In Namibia, Afrikaans, Ovambo, German, Herero, and English are widely spoken and understood. South Africa has 11 official languages, although English is the lingua franca except in the deepest rural areas. Zimbabwe and Botswana each have two or three

SOUTH AFRICAN WORDS & PHRASES

Biltong	Cured and dried meat
Boerewors (boerie)	South African sausage
Braai	Barbecue
Dagha boy	Old buffalo bull
Ellie	Elephant
Howzit?	Hello (how is it?)
Ja	Yes
Kikoi	Colorful wraparound sarong
Koppie/kopje	Small hill, usually a granite inselberg
Lekker	Nice/good
Mozzie	Mosquito
Mush/mushie	Nice/good
Mzungu/mlungu	A white person

SWAHILI WORDS & PHRASES

Basics

Yes	Ndio
No	Hapana
Please	Tafadhali
Thank you (very much)	Asante (sana)
You're welcome	Karibu
Hello	Jambo or hujambo
Good-bye	Kwaheri
How are you?	Habari?

Fine	Mzuri
Bad	Mbaya
So-so	Hivi hivi
Excuse me	Samahani
Doctor	Daktari
Medicine	Dawa

Food & Drink

Food	Chakula
Water	Maji
Bread	Mkate
Fruit(s)	(Ma)tunda
Vegetable	Mboga
Salt	Chumvi
Sugar	Sukari
Coffee	Kahawa
Tea	Chai
Beer	Pombe

Useful Phrases

What is your name?	Jina lako nani?
My name is . . .	Jina langu ni . . .
Where are you from?	Unatoka wapi?
I come from . . .	Mimi ninatoka . . .
Do you speak English?	Una sema kiingereza?
I don't speak Swahili.	Sisemi kiswahili.
I don't understand.	Sifahamu.

How do you say this in English?	Unasemaje kwa kiingereza?
How many?	Ngapi?
How much is it?	Ngapi shillings?
May I take your picture?	Mikupige picha?
Where is the bathroom?	Choo kiko wapi?
I need . . .	Mimi natafuta . . .
I want to buy . . .	Mimi nataka kununua . . .

ZULU WORDS & PHRASES

Basics

Yes	Yebo
No	Cha
Please	Ngicela
Thank you (very much)	Ngiyabonga
You're welcome	Nami ngiyabonga
Hello/good morning	Sawubona
Good day (reply to *good morning*)	Yebo, sawubona
Good-bye (go well)	Hamba kahle
How are you?	Usaphila?
I am well	Ngisaphila
I am ill	Ngiyagula
Excuse me	Uxolo
Doctor	Udokotela
Medicine	Umuthi

Food & Drink

Food	Ukudla
Water	Amanzi
Bread	Isinkwa
Fruit	Isithelo
Vegetable	Uhlaza
Salt	Usawoti
Sugar	Ushekela
Coffee	Ikhofi
Tea	Itiye
Beer	Utshwala

Useful phrases

What is your name?	Ubani igama lakho?
My name is . . .	Igama lami ngingu . . .
Do you speak English?	Uya khuluma isingisi?
I don't understand what you're saying.	Angizwa ukuthi uthini
How much is this?	Kuyimalini lokhu?
Where is the bathroom/toilet?	Likuphi itholethe?
I would like . . .	Ngidinga . . .
I want to buy . . .	Ngicela . . .

prevalent local languages, but English is the official one and widely understood. Zambia, Malawi, Kenya, Tanzania, and Uganda have many local languages, but again English is the most widely used and spoken, with Swahili being the common local lingo.

For the purpose of safaris, mastering the basics of just two foreign languages, Zulu and Swahili, should make you well equipped for travel through much of the region. Zulu is the most common of the Southern African Nguni family of languages (Zulu, Shangaan, Ndebele, Swazi, Xhosa), and is understood in South Africa and Zimbabwe. Swahili is a mixture of Arabic and Bantu and is used across East Africa. In Namibia, Botswana, Zambia, and Malawi your best bet initially is to stick with English.

Resources

Abercrombie & Kent International
www.abercrombiekent.com
1520 Kensington Rd.,
Suite 212
Oak Brook, IL 60521
Tel. 800/323–7308
Fax 818/507–5802

The Africa Adventure Company
www.africa-adventure.com
5353 N. Federal Highway,
Suite 300
Fort Lauderdale, FL 33308

Tel. 800/882–9453
Fax 954/491–9060

Africa Tours Inc.
www.africasafaris.com
217 Merrick Rd., Suite 212
Amityville, NY 11701
Tel. 800/235–3692
Fax 631/264–2801

African Travel Inc.
www.africantravelinc.com
1100 E. Broadway
Glendale, CA 91205
Tel. 800/444–2874
Fax 818/507–5802

Big Five Tours & Expeditions
www.bigfive.com
1551 S.E. Palm Ct.

Stuart, FL 34994
Tel. 800/244–3483
Fax 561/287–5990

Elderhostel
www.elderhostel.org
Tel. 877/426–8056

**Karell's African
Dream Vacations**
www.karell.com
814 Ponce De Leon Blvd.
Coral Gables, FL 33134
Tel. 305/446–7766
Fax 305/446–8553

Ker & Downey
www.kerdowney.com
6703 Highway Blvd.
Katy, TX 77494
Tel. 800/423–4236
Fax 281/371–2514

Park East Tours
www.parkeast.com
100 Environs Park
Helena, AL 35080
Tel. 800/223–6078
Fax 205/428–1714

Premier Tours
www.premiertours.com
1430 Walnut St., 2nd fl.
Philadelphia, PA 19102
Tel. 800/545–1910
Fax 215/893–0357

Reservations Africa
www.reservationsafrica.com
300–31 Bastion Sq.
Victoria, BC, Canada
V8W 1J1
Tel. 888/891–5111
Fax 250/386–3266

Travcoa
www.travcoa.com
2424 S.E. Bristol St.
Newport Beach, CA 92660
Tel. 800/992–2003
Fax 949/476–2583

**United Touring
International**
www.unitedtour.com
1 Bala Plaza, Suite 414
Bala Cynwyd, PA 19004
Tel. 800/223–6486
Fax 610/617–3312

Wildlife Safaris
www.wildlife-safari.com
346 Rheem Blvd., # 107
Moraga, CA 94556
Tel. 800/221–8118
Fax 925/376–5059

AFRICAN AIR CONSOLIDATORS

Air consolidators specialize
in bulk air-ticket sales to
the African continent.
Their rates are generally
less expensive than those
quoted by the airlines and,
in many cases, are equal to
or lower than fares offered
on the Internet.

African Travel Inc.
www.africantravelinc.com
1100 E. Broadway
Glendale, CA 91205
Tel. 800/444–2874
Fax 818/507–5802

Karrell's African Dream Vacations

www.karell.com
814 Ponce De Leon Blvd.
Coral Gables, FL 33134
Tel. 305/446–7766
Fax 305/446–8553

Magical Holidays

501 Madison Ave.
New York, NY 10022
Tel. 800/228–2208
Fax 212/486–9751

Premier Tours

www.premiertours.com
1430 Walnut St., 2nd fl.
Philadelphia, PA 19102
Tel. 800/545–1910
Fax 215/893–0357

AFRICA-BASED SAFARI OUTFITTERS

A number of these outfitters also own or manage camps and lodges in various countries.

Conservation Corporation (CCAfrica)

www.ccafrica.com
Tel. 27/11–809–4300

High-end lodges in South Africa, Zimbabwe, Namibia, Kenya, and Tanzania.

Desert & Delta Safaris

www.desertdelta.co.za
Tel. 27/11–706–0861

Chobe Game Lodge, Camp Moremi, as well as other high-end Botswana lodges.

Drifters Adventours

www.drifters.co.za
Tel. 27/11–888–1160

Mainly budget overland trips with some budget accommodations in South Africa, Namibia (Swakopmund), Zimbabwe (Victoria Falls), and Botswana (Maun).

Karibu Safaris

www.karibu.co.za
Tel. 27/31–563–9774

Mainly has lodges in Lower Zambezi National Park in Zambia, but also runs overland trips.

Landela Safaris

www.landela.co.zw
Tel. 263/4–73–4043

Lodges in Zimbabwe and Botswana.

Moremi Safaris & Tours

www.moremi-safaris.com
Tel. 27/11–465–3842

Trips to Botswana's Kalahari region to see traditional San hunter-gatherers.

Penduka Safaris

www.penduka.com.na
Tel. 264/61–239–643

Specialist in Kalahari overland trips.

Touch the Wild

www.touchthewild.co.za
Tel. 27/827–846–760

Tented camps and permanent lodges in Zimbabwe and Zambia.

Wild Frontiers

www.wildfrontiers.com
Tel. 27/11–702–2035
Fax 27/11–468–1655

Hiking, climbing, biking, rafting, and other adventure tours throughout Africa.

Wilderness Safaris

www.wilderness-safaris.co.za

(Accommodations can be booked only through an African tour operator or travel agent.)

Owns and runs highly regarded lodges in the best game areas in Botswana, Namibia, Zimbabwe, and Malawi. Also runs mobile and overland trips.

SAFARI CAMPS & LODGES

The following safari camps and lodges are mentioned in various locations throughout the book. A number of the companies listed have other properties that are not mentioned here.

CCAfrica

www.ccafrica.com
Box 16336
Vlaeberg 8018
Cape Town, South Africa
Tel. 27/11–809–4300

Among its extensive portfolio of high-end, highly regarded properties are Londolozi Game Reserve in South Africa and Ngorongoro Crater Lodge, Klein's Camp, and Grumeti River Camp in Tanzania.

Cottar's 1920s Camp

www.cottars.com
Tel. 888/870–0903

Luxurious small lodge in Kenya's Masai Mara.

Elephant Watch Safari Camp

www.olerai.com
Tel. 254/2–334–868

Small private lodge in Northern Kenya near an elephant research center.

Gametrackers (aka Orient Express Safaris)

www.orient-express-safaris.com
Box 786432
Sandton 2146
South Africa
Tel. 27/11–481–6052

High-end lodges in and around the Okavango Delta in Botswana.

Hamilton's Camp
www.threecities.co.za
Tel. 27/31–310–6900

Private concession in Kruger National Park run by South Africa–based Three Cities hotel group.

Jock Safari Lodge
www.jocksafarilodge.com
Tel. 27/13–735–5200

A private concession in Kruger National Park.

Lion Sands
www.lionsands.com
Tel./fax 27/13–735–5000

Small, midprice lodge in the exclusive Sabi Sand area of South Africa.

Lobo Wildlife Lodge
www.africanencounters.com
Postnet Suite 45, Private Bag X12, Roosevelt Park 2129 Johannesburg
Tel. 27/11–880–3079
Fax 27/11–447–6773

Low-end hotel-style lodge run by the government of Tanzania.

Mala Mala Game Reserve
www.malamala.com
Tel. 27/11–268–2388

In the Sabi Sand area of South Africa; this is the oldest photo-safari lodge in Africa as well as one of South Africa's most popular private lodges.

Norfolk Hotel
www.lonrhohotels.com
Tel. 254/2–216–940

An elegant, colonial-style property in Nairobi, Kenya.

Sabi Sabi Game Reserve
www.sabisabi.com
Tel. 27/11–483–3939

Luxury, private lodge in the Sabi Sand area of South Africa.

Sambiya Lodge
afritour@africaonline.co.ug
Tel. 256/41–233–596

Thatched-cottage camp in the Murchison Falls area of Uganda.

Sand River Selous Lodge
www.sandrivers.com/thelodge

(Accommodations can be booked only through an African-tour operator or travel agent.)

Small, upscale lodge in an area of Tanzania known for walking safaris.

Sanyanti Lodge
www.sanyati.com
Tel. 263/91–60–4231

Rustic lodge at Lake Kariba in Zimbabwe.

Sarova Paraa Lodge
reservations@sarova.com
Tel. 256/41–342–196

Midsize lodge in the Murchison Falls area of Uganda.

Serena Hotels
www.serenahotels.com
Tel. 254/2–711–077

Relatively large chain of hotels and lodges in Kenya and Tanzania.

Seronera Wildlife Lodge
Box 3100, Arusha,Tanzania
Tel. 255/57–2711
Fax 255/57–8502

Large lodge in the Serengeti Plains of Tanzania. It's easiest to book this remote lodge through a safari specialist.

Singita Game Reserve
www.singita.co.za
Tel. 27/11–234–0990

In the Sabi Sand area of South Africa, this upscale lodge is one of the most luxurious in Africa.

Sopa Hotels
www.sopalodges.com
Tel. 255/57–6886, 255/57–6896, or 254/2–336–088

Relatively large hotel and lodge chain in Kenya and Tanzania.

Stanley Hotel
www.sarovahotels.com
Tel. 254/2–228–830 or 254/2–333–233

One of the oldest hotels in Nairobi, Kenya.

Tswalu Private Kalahari Reserve
www.tswalu.com
Tel. 27/53–781–9311 or 27/53–781–9234

Private lodge and reserve bordering the Kalahari region of South Africa.

White Horse Inn
utb@starcom.co.ga
Tel. 256/48–623–336
Fax 256/48–623–717

The starting point for many of the treks to the gorilla sanctuaries in the Bwindi area of Uganda.

Zimbabwe Sun Hotels
www.zimsun.co.zw
Tel. 263/4–73–7944

Includes the Hwange Safari Lodge and Victoria Falls Hotels.

South African National Parks

Kruger National Park and Kgalagadi Transfrontier Park
www.parks-sa.co.za
Tel. 27/12–428–9111

Hluhluwe–Umfolozi Park
www.kznwildlife.com
Tel. 27/33–845–1000

Namibia Wildlife National Parks

Etosha National Park & Skeleton Coast National Park
www.namibweb.com/resorts.htm

Camel Safaris

Camel Trek (Kenya)
Tel. 254/2–89–1079
Fax 254/2–89–1716

Desert Rose Camels (Kenya)
Tel. 254/2–22–8936
Fax 254/2–22–2160

ReitSafari (Namibia)
www.reitsafari.com
Box 20706, Windhoek
Tel. 264/61–25–0764
Fax 264/61–25–6300

Elephant Safaris

Abu's Camp (Botswana)
www.elephantbacksafaris.com
Tel. 267/686–1260

Kapama Private Reserve (South Africa)
www.kapama.co.za
Tel. 27/12–804–4804

Wild Horizons (Zimbabwe)
www.wildhorizons.co.zw
Tel. 263/13–2313 or 263/13–2001

Or contact Wild Frontiers.
www.wildfrontiers.com
Tel. 27/11–702–2035
Fax 27/11–468–1655

Horse Safaris

Equus Safaris (South Africa)
www.explore-southafrica.co.za/explore/horse/equus
Tel. 27/11–788–3923

Macateers Horse Safaris (Botswana)
c/o Legendary Adventure Company, Box 40, Maun, Botswana
Tel. 267/660–211
Fax 267/660–379

Nyika Plateau Horse Safaris (Malawi)
www.nyika.com
Tel. 265/33–0180

Offbeat Horse Safaris (Kenya)
www.offbeatsafaris.com
Tel. 254/2–571–649 or 254/2–571–661

Okavango Horse Safaris (Botswana)
www.okavangohorse.com
Tel. 267/686–1671

ReitSafari (Namibia)
www.reitsafari.com
Box 20706, Windhoek
Tel. 264/61–25–0764
Fax 264/61–25–6300

Sun Seekers (South Africa)
Box 348, Hluhluwe, 3960, South Africa
Tel./fax 27/35–562–0337

Uto Farms Horse Trails (Tanzania)
www.wildfrontiers.com
Tel. 27/11–702–2035
Fax 27/11–468–1655

Walking Safaris

Chipembere Safaris (Zimbabwe)
chipsaf@Zambezi.net
Box 9, Kariba
Tel./fax 263/61–2946

Kruger Park Wilderness Trails (South Africa)
www.parks-sa.co.za
Tel. 27/12–428–9111

Mana Pools (Zimbabwe)
c/o Wild Africa Safaris
www.wildfrontiers.com
Tel. 27/11–702–2035
Fax 27/11–468–1655
Or contact Nature Ways Safaris.
natureways@zol.co.zw

Robin Pope Safaris (Zambia)
www.robinpopesafaris.net
Box 80, Mfuwe, Zambia

Sand River Selous (Tanzania)
c/o Falcon Africa Safaris
Box 3490, Randburg, 2125
Tel. 27/11–886–1938
Fax 27/11–886–1778

Umfolozi Wilderness Trails (South Africa)
Tel. 27/33–147–1981
Fax 27/33–147–1980

AMERICAN EMBASSIES IN AFRICA

Botswana
ConsularGaboro@state.gov
Embassy Enclave, Gabarone
Tel. 267/395–3982
Fax 267/395–6947

Kenya
info@kenyaembassy.com
Mombasa Rd., Nairobi
Tel. 254/2–537–800
Fax. 254/2–537–810

Namibia

www.usembassy.namib.com
Ausplan Bldg., 14 Lossen
St., Windhoek
Tel. 264/61–22–1601
Fax 264/61–22–9792

South Africa

pretoria.usembassy.gov
877 Pretorius St., Pretoria
Tel. 27/12–342–1048
Fax 27/12–342–2244

Tanzania

balozi@tanzaniaembassy-us.
org
140 Msese Rd., Kinondoni
District, Dar es Salaam
Tel. 255/51–666–010
Fax 255/51–666–701

Uganda

usembassy.state.gov/kampala
Parliament Ave., Kampala
Tel. 256/41–259–791
Fax 256/41–259–794

Zambia

lusaka.usembassy.gov
Independence and United
Nations Aves., Lusaka
Tel. 260/1–250–955
Fax 260/1–252–225

Zimbabwe

zimemb@erols.com
172 Herbert Chitepo Ave.,
Harare
Tel. 263/4–250–593
Fax 263/4–796–488

AFRICAN EMBASSIES IN THE UNITED STATES

Botswana

1608 New Hampshire Ave.
NW
Washington, DC 20036
Tel. 202/244–4990
Fax 202/244–4164

Kenya

www.kenyaembassy.com
2249 R St. NW
Washington, DC 20008
Tel. 202/387–6101
Fax 202/462–3829

Malawi

2408 Massachusetts Ave. NW
Washington, DC 20008
Tel. 202/797–1007

Namibia

1605 New Hampshire
Ave. NW
Washington, DC 20009
Tel. 202/986–0540
Fax 202/986–0443

South Africa

www.saembassy.org
3051 Massachusetts Ave. NW
Washington, DC 20008
Tel. 202/232–4400
Fax 202/244–9417

Tanzania

www.tanzaniaembassy-us.
org
2139 R St. NW
Washington, DC 20008
Tel. 202/939–6125
Fax 202/797–7408

Uganda
5911 16th St. NW
Washington, DC 20011
Tel. 202/726–7100
Fax 202/726–1727

Zambia
www.zambiaembassy.org
2419 Massachusetts
Ave. NW
Washington, DC 20008
Tel. 202/265–9717
Fax 202/332–0826

Zimbabwe
www.zimembassy-usa.org
1531–33 New Hampshire
Ave. NW
Washington, DC 20009
Tel. 202/483–9326
Fax 202/483–9326

MORE INFORMATION ABOUT AFRICA

Regional Tourism Organization of Southern Africa (RETOSA)
www.retosa.co.za
Box 7381, Halfway House
Johannesburg 1685, South
Africa
Tel. 27/11–31–52420 or
27/11–31–52422

Represents the tourism
interests of Botswana,
Malawi, Namibia, South
Africa, Tanzania, Zambia,
and Zimbabwe.

AIRLINES

British Airways (BA; operating as Comair in Africa)
www.british-airways.com
Tel. 800/247–9297; 416/250–
0880 in Canada; 011/921–
0222 in South Africa

Delta Air Lines (DL)
www.delta.com
Tel. 800/221–1212; 800/231–
0856 international; 800/
525–0280 in Canada; 404/
715–1450 customer service

KLM (KL)
www.klm.com
Tel. 800/447–4747 in U.S.
and Canada

Lufthansa (LH)
www.lufthansa.com
Tel. 800/645–3880; 800/563–
5954 in Canada

Nationwide
www.flynationwide.co.za
Tel. 877/759–9711

South African Airways (SA)
www.flysaa.com
Tel. 800/722–9675; 800/387–
4629 in Canada; 011/978–
1111 in South Africa

Virgin Atlantic Airways (VS)
www.virgin-atlantic.com
Tel. 800/862–8621;
1293/450–150 in U.K.

AIRPORTS

Atlanta (ATL)
www.atlanta-airport.com

Cape Town (CPT)
www.airports.co.za/acsa/cia/cia_home.html

Johannesburg (JNB)
www.airports.co.za/acsa/jia/jia_home.html

Nairobi (NBO)
www.meteo.go.ke/obsv/stations/jomo.html

**New York
John F. Kennedy (JFK)**
www.panynj.gov/aviation/jfkframe.htm

HEALTH & OTHER USEFUL INFORMATION

American Society of Tropical Medicine and Hygiene
www.astmh.org
60 Revere Dr., Suite 500
Northbrook, IL 60062
Tel. 847/480–9592

Centers for Disease Control and Prevention (CDC)
cdc.gov
1600 Clifton Rd.
Atlanta, GA 30333
Tel. 800/311–3435 general information; 877/394–8747 traveler information

Foreign and Commonwealth Office
fco.gov.uk

Travel tips for areas worldwide.

International Association for Medical Assistance to Travelers
iamat.org
U.S. Headquarters
417 Center St.
Lewiston, NY 14092
Tel. 716/754–4883

International Society of Travel Medicine
www.istm.org

International SOS Assistance
internationalsos.com
8 Neshaminy Interplex, Suite 207
Trevose, PA 19053-6956
Tel. 215/244–1500 or 800/523–8930

Global emergency assistance and travel health policies, as well as trip-cancellation and trip-interruption coverage.

Medical Advisory Services for Travelers Abroad (MASTA)
www.masta.org
Moorfield Rd.
Yeadon, Leeds
Great Britain LS19 7BN
Tel. 44–0–113–38–7575

NetCare Travel Clinics
www.travelclinic.co.za

Africa-specific health Web site with tips on everything from eclipse watching to malaria prevention.

Overseas Citizens Services
travel.state.gov
U.S. Department of State
Tel. 202/647–5225 travel warnings; 888/407–4747 emergency; 317/472–2328 emergency from overseas

World Health Organization
who.int
525 23rd St. NW
Washington, DC 20037
Tel. 202/861–3200

Worldwide Assistance
www.worldwideassistance.com
1133 15th St. NW, Suite 400
Washington, DC 20005
Tel. 800/777–8710 Ext. 417; 703/204–1897 or 800/821–2828 for enrollment

GENERAL INTERNATIONAL TRAVEL INFORMATION

Federal Consumer Information Center
pueblo.gsa.gov
Pueblo, CO 81009 Tel. 800/333–4636

Information on entry requirements to various countries, including passport requirements.

Overseas Citizens Services
U.S. Department of State
travel.state.gov
Tel. 202/647–5225

U.S. Customs Service
www.customs.ustreas.gov/travel/travel.htm
Box 7407
Washington, DC 20044

Links to useful publications, such as the fact-packed "Know Before You Go," mandatory reading if you're headed overseas.

U.S. Department of State
travel.state.gov
Tel. 900/225–5674 or 888/362–8668

Information about passports and security abroad. The 900 number is a toll call; the 888 number is toll free, but you need a credit card to obtain further information. You can download a passport application from the Web site; a live operator can tell you the status of your application (for a fee).

V.A.T. Refunds
Global Refund
www.globalrefund.com
99 Main St., Suite 307
Nyack, NY 10960
Tel. 845/348–7673 or
800/566–9828

SAFARI CLOTHING & RESOURCES

Eastern Mountain Sports
www.emsonline.com
Tel. 888/463–6367
Fax 603/924–4320

Outdoor gear retailer with
an online catalog and stores
nationwide.

Ex Officio
exofficio.com
Tel. 800/644–7303

Online clothing company
with clothing and gear for
adventure travel and excursions in harsh weather.

Lands' End
www.landsend.com
Tel. 800/332–0103

General travel clothes and
supplies.

Magellan's
magellans.com
Tel. 800/962–4943

Range of travel items from
jet-lag-prevention medicine
to outdoor wear.

Patagonia
www.patagonia.com
Tel. 800/638–6464; 800/336–
9090 catalog requests

Manufacturer of outdoor
gear, including luggage,
backpacks, and accessories,
with retail stores and online
and mail-order catalogs.

REI
www.rei.com
Tel. 253/891–2500 or
800/426–4840
Fax 253/891–2523

Manufacturer of outdoor
gear and clothing with retail
stores and catalog, and
online sales.

Russell Friedman Books
www.rfbooks.co.za

African natural-history
book specialist with titles
on birds, plants, insects,
wildlife, conservation, and
ecology.

Tag Safari Travel Clothing
www.tagsafari.com

Safari clothing manufactured
in Zimbabwe and distributed
in the United States through
Houston headquarters.

Tilley Endurables
www.tilley.com
900 Don Mills Rd.
Toronto, ON, Canada
M3C 1V6
Tel. 416/441–6141 or
800/363–8737

High-performance travel
clothing; most items dry
overnight even under humid
conditions.

PASSPORTS & VISAS

**American Passport
Service**
www.americanpassport.com
10 Vaughan Mall
Portsmouth, NH 03801
Tel. 603/431–8482 or
800/841–6778

Express Visa Services
www.expressvisa.com
18 E. 41st St., Suite 1206
New York, NY 10017
Tel. 212/679–5650

Seven locations around the
United States process visas.

National Passport Center
www.travel.state.gov/
passport_services.html
Tel. 877/487–2778

Passport Express
www.passportexpress.com
179 Wayland Ave.
Providence, RI 02906
Tel. 401/272–4612 or
800/362–8196

Travisa
www.travisa.com
Tel. 800/222–2589 or
800/421–5468

Issues passports and visas in
24 hours.

**U.S. Department
of State**
www.travel.state.gov
Tel. 202/647–5225

Publishes a number of
useful information sheets,
including consular information on many countries. Also
good: "Your Trip Abroad,"
"A Safe Trip Abroad," and
various tip sheets for
regional travel.

TRAVEL INSURANCE

**Travel Guard
International**
www.travel-guard.com
1145 Clark St.
Stevens Point, WI 54481
Tel. 800/826–4919

WEATHER

CNN Weather
www.cnn.com/weather

Weather Channel
www.weather.com

What to Read Before You Go

BOOKS

Africa

African Game Trails,
Theodore Roosevelt

*A Bushveld Safari: A Young
Explorer's Guide to the
Bushveld,* Nadine Clarke

Coming Back to Earth, James
Clarke

Flame Trees of Thika,
Elspeth Huxley
(autobiography)

*The Game Rangers: 78
authentic stories from the
African bush,* Jan Rodrigues

*The Great Safari: The Lives
of George and Joy Adamson,*
Adrian House (biography)

*Happy Valley, the History
of the English in Kenya,*
Nicholas Best (history)

I Dreamed of Africa,
Kuki Gallman
(autobiography)

Jock of the Bushveld,
Sir Percy Fitzpatrick

Man-eaters of Tsavo, Colonel
Patterson (autobiography)

*Natural Selections:
the African Wanderings
of a Bemused Naturalist,*
Don Pinnock

Nine Faces of Kenya,
compiled by Elspeth Huxley

Out of Africa, Isak Dinesen
(a.k.a. Karen Blixen)

Running the Gauntlet,
George Mossop

Serengeti Shall Not Die,
Bernard Grzimek
(autobiography)

Silence Will Speak, Errol
Trzebinski (biography)

*South African Eden: the
Kruger National Park, 1902–
1946,* James Stevenson-
Hamilton

West with the Night, Beryl
Markham (autobiography)

*White Mischief: The Murder
of Lord Erroll,* James Fox
(biography)

Animals

Among the Elephants,
Iain Douglas-Hamilton
(Northern Kenya)

Cats of Africa,
Anthony Hall-Martin
(Southern Africa)

*Coming of Age with
Elephants,* Joyce Poole
(Amboseli, Kenya)

Elephants of Africa,
Anthony Hall-Martin
(Southern Africa)

Elephant Memories, Cynthia
Moss (Amboseli, Kenya)

Portraits of the Wild, Cynthia
Moss (Amboseli, Kenya)

The Serengeti Lion,
George Schaller
(Serengeti, Tanzania)

Solo, An African Wild Dog,
Hugo Van Lawick
(Serengeti, Tanzania)

Through a Window,
Jane Goodall (Tanzania)

Field Guides

*A Field Guide to the Birds of
East Africa,* John G. Williams
and Norman Arlott

*A Field Guide of the Larger
Mammals of Africa,* Jean
Dorst and Pierre Dandelot

*A Field Guide to the National
Parks of East Africa,* John G.
Williams and Norman Arlott

*The Kingdon Field Guide to
African Mammals,* Jonathon
Kingdon

*The Safari Companion:
A Guide to Watching African
Mammals,* Richard D. Estes

*Signs of the Wild: A field
guide to the spoor and signs of
the mammals of southern
Africa,* Clive Walker

Photographic Safaris

Africa's Big Five, William Taylor, Gerald Hinde, Richard du Toit

African Predators, Guss Mills and Martin Harvey

Other Titles

Fodor's Southern Africa, Fodor's Travel Publications

Guide's Guide to Guiding, Garth Thompson

Traveller's Health, Dr. Richard Dawood

Index